God's Design for Broken Lives

··

Rebuilding after Divorce

··

Barbara Dycus

CHRISM

Springfield, Missouri
02-0344

Some of the concepts in chapter 13 are taken from chapter 3, "The Seasons of Divorce," in Jim and Barbara Dycus, *Children of Divorce* (Elgin, Ill.: David C. Cook Publishing Co., 1987).

Every effort has been made to trace copyright holders—without results in a few instances. This will be rectified in future editions if the relevant information can be obtained.

Chrism books are published by Gospel Publishing House.

Library of Congress Cataloging-in-Publication Data

Dycus, Barbara.
    God's design for broken lives: rebuilding after divorce / Barbara Dycus.
        p.   cm.
    ISBN 0-88243-344-X
        1. Divorced people—Religious life.   2. Divorce—Religious aspects—Christianity. I. Title.
    BV4596.D58D83   1994
    248.8'46—dc20   94-8615

Printed in the United States of America

For those who have experienced brokenness through divorce

Table of Contents

Preface

Two words changed my life for all time: "I'm leaving."

I heard my father say those words one day as he walked down the stairs of our home with two suitcases in his hands. Those words ended a marriage that had begun almost twenty-five years earlier. With those words, I became a child of divorce.

The emotional upheaval divorce brought to my life would affect me for many years. It affects me yet today. My teen years became the most confusing, soul-searching period of my life. But with the foundation of faith that my parents had instilled in me, I was able to turn the negative effect of that experience into a positive thrust for my life's purpose. I would not be writing this book if I had not experienced my parents' divorce. Nor would I be involved in ministry to children of divorce and their parents.

My parents were devastated by their crisis. Active Christians in our little church, my father had served as Sunday school superintendent and my mother had been very involved with the women's ministries. But both of them felt their divorce had removed them from God's favor. They were unable to prepare my sister or me in any way for the changes the divorce would bring.

The small conservative church we attended was unable to accept this fall from God's standards and asked our family to leave the congregation. And so we did, never to return.

7

Twelve years later, while serving God in full-time ministry, I fell in love with and married my husband, Jim. That was just one and a half years after his conversion from seventeen years of heroin addiction. During the years before his conversion Jim had married and divorced—not once, but four times.

Again, divorce was affecting my life. The denomination in which I was involved in full-time ministry asked me to give up my ministry when I married a divorced man. But God called us into a new ministry, and Jim became an associate pastor in our present denomination. His ministerial ordination is with yet another organization, which has no restrictions against credentialing a divorced person.

In Chicago we began to see more and more divorced people visit the church and then leave. We asked, "What are we doing to meet their needs right where they are?" We both had heard plenty of teaching on how God hates divorce, but little or nothing about how God loves and wants to heal a family broken by divorce.

We asked God to help us design just such a ministry. He directed us to John 8, the story of the woman taken in adultery, and John 4, the account of Jesus with the woman at the well. In both cases His approach was one of compassion and concern. He accepted the women just as they were; His greatest concern was for their present condition, not their past mistakes.

We asked God: "Give us the divorced for our inheritance!" It was then that we founded Support Ministries, focusing on helping both divorcing and divorced adults and their children.

In more than twenty years we have seen thousands of divorced persons made whole again by the touch of God in their lives. Their marriages weren't always put back together, but their lives were directed back to God's divine plan for them. They moved from devastating hurt to healing and recovery.

This book is the culmination of twenty years of ministry to these individuals. Twice a year we offer support workshops where this information is presented to adults, while complementary workshops offer age-appropriate information to their children.

As a young pastor's wife just beginning ministry to divorced persons, I was greatly influenced by a book called *Forgiving Is For Giving* by Harold Ivan Smith, written under the pen name

Jason Towner. Thank you, Harold. Chapter 7 of this book has evolved from seed thoughts planted by your book.

Introduction

Welcome to *God's Design for Broken Lives.*

One of the most important lessons in life that we can learn is this: Brokenness is the first step to wholeness!

Most of us are familiar with brokenness. Broken homes, broken marriages, broken family structures, and broken hopes and dreams seem to plague humanity today. This brokenness in relationships destroys lives and paralyzes emotions. Brokenness robs us of our hope!

My message to you through the chapters of this book is one of hope in a world shrouded with hopelessness. Our hope comes because we serve a God who finds delight in taking broken lives and bringing them into the beauty of the wholeness He designed them to experience.

Think for a moment of Abraham. God had promised him he would become the "father of many nations" (Genesis 17:4). Yet, year after empty year passed without a child. Finally, in their old age, Abraham and Sarah became the parents of Isaac. What joy and happiness that little boy must have brought to his parents! God's promise had come true. God had kept His word. This little miracle child was the hope of their future.

Then that fateful day came when God asked Abraham to take this precious son, this miracle child, and literally offer him as a sacrifice. Could Abraham do it? (Could you?) Because of his success in handling a personal crisis, Abraham leaves us a pattern for turning brokenness into wholeness.

The apostle Paul said of Abraham, referring to this time of distress: "[Abraham], who against hope believed in hope . . . staggered not at the promise of God through unbelief; but was strong in faith, giving glory to God; and being fully persuaded, that what he had promised, he was able also to perform" (Romans 4:18,20–21, KJV).

And Alan Redpath, in *Victorious Christian Living,* makes this observation:

> There is nothing—no circumstance, no trouble, no testing—that can ever touch me until, first of all, it has gone past God and past Christ, right through to me. If it has come that far, it has come with a great purpose, which I may not understand at the moment; but as I refuse to become panicky, as I lift my eyes up to him and accept it as coming from the throne of God for some great purpose of blessing to my own heart, no sorrow will ever disturb me, no trial will ever disarm me, no circumstance will cause me to fret, for I shall rest in the joy of what my Lord is. That is the rest of victory.

It takes courage to trust God—to walk with Him through brokenness to wholeness. But God has a design for your life that is unaltered by any of life's circumstances, untouched by brokenness, which He longs to share with you.

Divorce has held so many people captive to their hurts. But God, by appropriating His grace to their hopeless situations, can set the captives free to experience wholeness and healing. His touch can take the broken pieces of their lives and put them back together in a beautiful design. Will you take God's hand and allow Him to lead you into His design for your life? He's waiting for you to do so. It's His promise to you:

> I know the plans I have for you . . . plans to prosper you and not to harm you, plans to give you hope and a future. Then you will call upon me and come and pray to me, and I will listen to you. You will seek me and find me when you seek me with all your heart. I will be found by you . . . and will bring you back from captivity (Jeremiah 29:11–14).

1

Good Grief

Chapter Focus

Our hope is that God has a better plan than to allow us to spend the rest of our days bearing the open wound of grief. We can learn to turn our grief into good grief.

What God's Word Says

"My life is consumed by anguish and my years by groaning; my strength fails because of my affliction, and my bones grow weak" (Psalm 31:10).

"Woe to me because of my injury! My wound is incurable! Yet I said to myself, 'This is my sickness, and I must endure it'" (Jeremiah 10:19).

Vignette

According to David and Joy Rice in *Living Through Divorce:*

In marriage one expects love, loyalty, and commitment from a highly invested love object. From the significant other, a person also expects to receive a basic confirmation of self-worth, ability to be loved, and life meaning. The dissolution of the bond and the explosion of the fantasy of marital continuance can generate intense feelings of betrayal, failure, and the loss of self-esteem. The greater the emotional investment in this dream, in marriage as an institution to fulfill personal identity, the greater the potential stress and conflict in divorce.

One dictionary defines grief this way: "Grief is emotional suffering caused by a loss or misfortune; deep sadness."

A man experiencing the grief of divorce put it this way: "My hands are shaky. I want to call her again but I know it's no good. She'll only yell and scream. It makes me feel lousy. I have work to do but I can't do it. I can't concentrate. I want to call people up, go see them, but I'm afraid they'll see that I'm shaky. But I just want to talk. I can't think about anything besides this trouble with Nina. I think I want to cry."

Maybe you have experienced this "deep sadness." Maybe you are still experiencing it, and in fact can't seem to move beyond it.

You aren't alone if you feel that way. Many thousands of people are living in grief-stricken, immobilizing sadness due to the loss of a loved one through divorce.

The prophet Jeremiah felt deep sadness. "Woe is me for my hurt! my wound is grievous. . . . Truly this is a grief, and I must bear it" (Jeremiah 10:19, KJV).

In the Chinese language, the word "crisis" has two characters: One meaning "danger," the other meaning "opportunity."

How do you view your crisis of loss? Is it "danger," or is it an opportunity for something new to happen in your life?

List the "danger" that grief and loss have brought to your life.

Now list the ways this experience can be viewed as an "opportunity."

14

In Psalm 31:10 David says, "My life is spent with grief" (KJV). Yet we know from the history of David's life that he learned to live through his grief and found God's restorative plan beyond his experience of grief.

How did he learn to do it? What caused his wound to heal? Is it possible that we can be healed in the same way?

In searching for the answers to these questions, we turn to Isaiah 53:3–4: "[Jesus was] a man of sorrows, and familiar with suffering. . . . *Surely he took up our infirmities and carried our sorrows*" (emphasis added).

Isaiah, Jeremiah, and David all learned to turn to God in their times of grieving. With His help they learned to grow through their season of grief and move on to the season of hope. "Then they cried to the Lord in their trouble, and he saved them from their distress" (Psalm 107:13).

As we learn to hand over our grief to Jesus and let Him bear it, He teaches us how to turn it into good grief. It becomes an opportunity for positive growth in our lives. Jesus was a crisis Teacher. He came to teach us how to live in hope. "The Spirit of the Lord is upon me, because he hath anointed me to preach the gospel to the poor; He hath sent me to heal the brokenhearted, to preach deliverance to the captives, and recovering of sight to the blind, to set at liberty them that are bruised, to preach the acceptable year of the Lord" (Luke 4:18–19, KJV).

Using the following letter form, write a letter to God, telling Him about your grief. Conclude your letter by handing your grief, once and for all, over to Jesus.

Dear God,

_____

_____

_____

_____

_____

_____

_____

In the remainder of this chapter we are going to take a close look at grief, particularly grieving itself. We will discover the causes of grief, its symptoms, and its stages, as well as set some goals to help in overcoming grief.

The Causes of Grief

I remember well one night of our single-parent family workshops when we were discussing the subject of grief. I asked the people in the room to briefly describe how they felt since their divorce had occurred.

Dick seemed to be struggling emotionally at having to describe his divorce experience. Several months earlier his wife had left him to raise his four small daughters. He was a kind, sensitive, Christian gentleman. I knew he struggled not only with the emotional hurts, but also with the guilt that he had failed at keeping one of God's standards. It came time for Dick to express his feelings. He paused for what seemed a long time, struggling to maintain his composure. Then he stated simply: "I feel robbed!"

How perfectly he had described not only his experience with loss, but every person's experience with this negative event. As he spoke, I thought back to when I was single, living alone in a high-rise apartment in Chicago. I came home late one night to discover the door of my apartment standing open. Feelings of loss, fear, anger, and helplessness swept over me at that instant. Those are the same feelings that linger for months following the loss of a loved one.

Let's consider some of the causes of grief:

• Loss of a love relationship

This is the most obvious cause of grief.

• Loss of future plans

It may be the failure to reach some goal for our lives, the loss of a gratifying job, the foreclosure of a home, or the missed opportunity to better ourselves. All such losses will signal the beginning of grief.

• Loss of status as a "couple"

A broken love relationship brings grief—not only because of the absence of that person, but also because of the sudden recognition that you are no longer a couple. It is not easy to adjust to being single again. A woman once said to me, "My husband has been gone for a year and a half, and I still detest that word *single!*"

• Loss of children or immediate family members

Many times divorce takes away more than a spouse. Close family members and friends, and even children, may suffer severed relationships.

Although there are other causes of grief, these are some of the major ones, signaling its onset.

Loss causes an imbalance in our security structure. At a time when our emotional tolerance is already low due to grief, we are called on to cope with the major changes that accompany divorce, such as moving, making explanations to our children, job hunting, and dealing with financial woes.

What are the causes of your grief?

What have you lost?

17

Grief is normal. It is important that we learn to see it as both normal and a process. Grief allows a person to disengage from the severed relationship and to find new, productive directions and goals for the future. Since grief is a process, it takes time to complete. As your body must heal following surgery, your emotions need to mend after divorce. Give yourself the time to heal.

The Symptoms of Grief

Has someone ever returned something to you that you didn't even realize you had lost? Even though you have that lost item in your hand, you still experience the feelings of loss, particularly if it was a valuable or prized object.

The arousal of feelings is evidence that the loss is recognized. It's like picking up a beautiful little baby and holding it close to you and then realizing that while the baby itself is as clean as the newly fallen snow—its diaper isn't.

So many times we don't understand the feelings we are experiencing. We condemn ourselves, saying, "I ought to know better than to feel that way!" Or, "If I were really as close to God as I say I am, I would be handling this better!"

I remember reading *Risky Living* by Jamie Buckingham. He compares life to a calm, serene lake with gentle breezes causing beautiful ripples on the surface. Suddenly the storm comes. It stirs up muck and mire that lie on the bottom of our lake.

"Where did that come from?" we ask in horror. The symptoms of grief may horrify us with their intensity. But just as the storms bring up the muck and mire, these normal feelings are surfacing so we can turn them over to God and lessen their impact.

Following are some of the symptoms that may surface during grieving.

18

•Regression

You may experience a real need to be cared for and held as a tiny infant. The child within you is in pain. It is a normal reaction for that child to reach out for nurturing and support in excessive amounts during this period.

•Anxiety

Anxiety is a reaction to the danger which the loss has brought. Along with it comes fear of a new and uncertain future.

•Anger and Resentment

This anger and resentment may be directed at others. It comes from your feelings of being deceived by life. This isn't how you imagined your life would be. Or your anger may be directed at yourself for not handling the situation better. You may feel upset that you let yourself get in this position.

•Guilt

Guilt is compounded for the Christian who is divorcing: guilt for having violated God's values and expectations as well as your own.

Guilt and anger are commonly recognized as ties to the past. They come from a negative response to grieving.

There are other milder symptoms, which are normal for the person in grief.

•Verbosity

You find yourself continually talking about your situation. Although this may not seem to be too big of a problem, it paralyzes you from moving beyond your grief to positive adjustment.

•Relational Difficulties

You fear being hurt again so you push people away. Then you pull them to you trying to fill the void in your life.

•Rapid Mood Changes

One moment you laugh, the next you cry. Little things upset you. Or you may laugh uproariously over nothing.

•Loss of Reality

You feel as though you are in a daze, unable to trust your feelings because you can't control them.

•Fantasies

You fantasize and imagine that you see or hear your lost

19

loved one. You think your heart has been ripped out and is missing.

•Loneliness

A deep sense of loneliness takes over your life.

•Depression

The symptoms of depression are lack of concentration, feelings of helplessness, guilt, and self-criticism.

•Suicidal Feelings

Many divorced persons admit to feelings of suicide at one point in their grieving.

If these are the symptoms of grief, how does one know when the process of grief is completed? One way is this—you suddenly realize you no longer have these symptoms. You can recall how you felt when you were experiencing them, but now you no longer feel that way.

Carefully consider each of these symptoms. Have you experienced these, and how did you feel as they surfaced in your emotions?

Regression

Anxiety

Anger and Resentment

Guilt

Verbosity

Relational Difficulties

Rapid Mood Changes

Loss of Reality

Fantasies

Loneliness

Depression

Suicidal Feelings

Have these symptoms begun to diminish in your emotions? Which are no longer difficult for you to control? Which do you still struggle to control?

The Stages of Grief

There are many different explanations of grieving. But in most cases a person will pass through the following stages.

•Denial

"This can't be happening to me!" "There's something I can do to change this." "I'm going to wake up tomorrow and this horrible experience will be gone!"

•Anger

When the realization hits us that this experience is not going to go away, anger often surfaces. Anger arises from thwarted goals. As we admit our anger, we move on to the next stage.

•Guilt

Often guilt is nothing more than anger turned inward. The guilt may be real or assumed, but we will have to pass through this stage of grieving.

•Bargaining

"I promise to do this, or be that . . . if only this situation will go away and bring my life back to normal again."

We may do some bargaining at all the various stages we pass through, but the final "bargain basement days" will be a time when we attempt to change the situation through some action on our part.

•Depression

If there is something good about depression, it is that we reach such a low there is only one way that we can go—up.

•Separation

We will never be able to concentrate on opening doors to the future if we haven't successfully closed the door on the past. Isaiah 43:18–19 tells us to "forget the former things; do not dwell on the past. See, I [God] am doing a new thing."

•Acceptance

Dr. Elisabeth Kübler-Ross wrote in her book *On Death and Dying,* "The harder they struggle to avoid the inevitable death, the more they try to deny it, the more difficult it will be for them to reach this final stage of acceptance with peace and dignity."

Not only must we reach an acceptance about the death of a relationship by divorce, but we must reach an acceptance of our lot in life at this time—acceptance of an altered, but promising future.

Describe your experience at each of these stages:

Denial

Anger

Guilt

Bargaining

Depression

Separation

Acceptance

How did you recognize that you had reached the acceptance stage?

There is one thing that is present through all these stages: *Hope!* "We have this hope as an anchor for the soul, firm and secure" (Hebrews 6:19). "You will keep in perfect peace him whose mind is steadfast, because he trusts in you" (Isaiah 26:3).

Setting Goals for Overcoming Grief

There are so many changes that occur during the process of grief that the decisions and changes may seem insurmountable.

Goals are a specific means of getting you where you want to go. They become your road map for the future. They bring you out of the past, remove the mire of the present, and make your future a reality.

The apostle Paul had a goal to remove the past from his present: "Not that I have already obtained all this, or have already been made perfect, but I press on to take hold of that for which

Christ Jesus took hold of me. Brothers, I do not consider myself yet to have taken hold of it. But one thing I do: forgetting what is behind and straining toward what is ahead, I press on toward the goal to win the prize for which God has called me heavenward in Christ Jesus" (Philippians 3:12–14).

The psalmist in Psalm 31 also recognized the value of goal-setting. In verse 10, David exclaims: "My life is spent with grief" (KJV).

With recognition of God's scriptural goals for his life, David overcame his grief. He is able to report (vv. 14,17): "I trust in you, O Lord. . . . You are my God. . . . I have cried out to You."

Let's see what these scriptural goals are:

• Make Him your God.

• Trust Him.

• Cry out to Him.

If we will do these three things, God promises to fulfill some of His own goals for our recovery period from grief:

• He provides for you.

"How great is your goodness which you have stored up for those who fear you, which you bestow . . . on those who take refuge in you" (v. 19).

• He protects you.

"In the shelter of your presence you hide them from the intrigues of men; in your dwelling you keep them safe from the strife of tongues" (v. 20).

• He preserves you.

"The Lord preserves the faithful, but the proud he pays back in full" (v. 23).

God will give you victory over grief.

Listen to these beautiful words from a Gaither song:

> Something beautiful, something good.
> All my confusion He understood.
> All I had to offer Him was brokenness and strife,
> But He made something beautiful of my life.

2

Overcoming Depression and Anger

Chapter Focus

Depression is a common state in today's society. It plagues sinner and saint alike. The key to ending depression lies in knowing what to do with the sense of emptiness it brings.

What God's Word Says

"I cry to you for help, O Lord; in the morning my prayer comes before you. Why, O Lord, do you reject me and hide your face from me? . . . You have taken my companions and loved ones from me; the darkness is my closest friend" (Psalm 88:13–14,18).

Vignette

In his book *Drumbeat of Love,* Lloyd John Ogilvie talks about the apostles during the ten days after the ascension of Jesus to heaven and before Pentecost. Listen to his description:

> The Lord is never nearer than when He excavates a sense of emptiness in us. The Holy Spirit can fill only empty hearts.
>
> The Apostles more than met this qualification as they waited in the Upper Room. Emptiness? They felt it with devastating insufficiency. They had experienced a life of high adventure with

Jesus. The power of God had been exposed in his message, healing, and love. Not even death could defeat that power. And Jesus had told them that that same power would be theirs. But now as they waited despairingly for the fulfillment of his promise of power, the words of hope seemed to mock their impotence and inadequacy. It's a terrible thing to have a passion with no power to live it out. Four words express the Apostles' emptiness prior to Pentecost: discouragement, dejection, disablement, and depression.

No wonder depression captured the emotions of Jesus' followers. It grew out of the desperate feeling that they could not be what they had been called to be.

What is depression? It is all of the following emotions and probably more:

•Pessimism

•Discouragement

•Dejection

•Apathy

•Despondency

•Preoccupation with life and misfortunes

•Contemplation of suicide

•Anguish

•Despair

•Self-disgust

•Intense guilt

•Anger

•Fear

•Hopelessness

Which of the emotions in the previous list are you currently experiencing?

What causes these feelings of depression? Is it . . .
- •trying to do your best and finding out it's not enough?
- •trying to make a difference, and finding out you haven't?
- •loving with all your heart, and knowing the love is not returned?

The feelings of the apostles in the Upper Room are common to us all.

In Psalm 88:1–9 we find a good example of depression. These nine verses of Scripture contain twenty-one complaints (feelings) of the psalmist.

Let's take a look at the psalmist's plea, while recognizing his complaints to God:

O Lord, the God who saves me, day and night I cry out before you. May my prayer come before you; turn your ear to my cry. For my soul is full of trouble and my life draws near the grave. I am counted among those who go down to the pit; I am like a man without strength. I am set apart with the dead, like the slain who lie in the grave, whom you remember no more, who are cut off from your care. You have put me in the lowest pit, in the darkest depths. Your wrath lies heavily upon me; you have overwhelmed me with all your waves. You have taken from me my closest friends and have made me repulsive to them. I am confined and cannot escape; my eyes are dim with grief. I call to you, O Lord, every day; I spread out my hands to you.

It is obvious that there was a deep sense of emptiness in the psalmist as he penned these words. As he contemplated his depressed feelings, he made one erroneous assumption that all mankind makes when depressed—He attributed his troubles to God!

Go over the passage above and circle the complaints that you, like the psalmist, have made.

Have you ever attributed your troubles to God? How?

Is God responsible for our troubles?

For an answer to that question let's look at one of the most important principles found in God's Word: "Do not be deceived: God cannot be mocked. A man reaps what he sows. The one who sows to please his sinful nature, from that nature will reap destruction; the one who sows to please the Spirit, from the Spirit will reap eternal life" (Galatians 6:7–8).

The only sense in which God is responsible for our troubles is in His having established the principle of sowing and reaping.

If we can't blame God for our troubles, then whom shall we blame? More to the point, if we can't blame our depression in response to our troubles on God, what is the source of depression?

Read what Ogilvie says: "I am convinced that depression is not circumstantial or environmental, but deeply personal. It is rage turned in upon ourselves as a result of the disturbing realization that we can't change things in ourselves, in people, or in situations."

Using that concept, let's develop a working definition of depression: "Depression principally is self-preoccupation—eyes turned inward on self. It comes as a result of a failure in self-control and self-discipline."

Talk about hitting a guy when he's down—that definition does! But the negatives about us can never be changed by ignoring them and hoping they will go away. We have to accept the negatives and face them before we can move away from them.

In Psalm 88 there are thirty-four personal pronouns. Thirty-four times the psalmist refers to himself.

That's self-preoccupation, isn't it?

Think about the things that cause depression in you. Write a narrative paragraph below describing your depression and the situation you feel caused it.

Now count the times that you have made a personal reference to yourself.

_____ personal references

Adding to the problem of depression for the Christian is guilt. Guilt comes from a failure to handle our problems God's way. All other attempts to treat our depression only compound the guilt and equal more depression.

By taking a look at three biblical characters who experienced periods of deep depression, we can discover ways to deal with our own times of depression. All three of these men became so depressed they thought physical death was their only solution. God met each of them and brought them back into hopeful, joyous futures.

He will do the same for you!

Moses: Learning Dependence on God

For the account of Moses and the circumstances leading up to his battle with depression we turn to the Book of Numbers. You will need to scan the first thirteen chapters to be aware of Moses' circumstances.

Moses was the man chosen by God to lead Israel out of bondage. He confronted Pharaoh twelve times before the people were allowed to leave. About three and a half million people followed his leadership out of Egypt.

Many supernatural confirmations of Moses' leadership took place in the early chapters of Numbers. Among them were

- the first Israelite census and establishment of twelve governing tribes
- the Levitical duties in the Tabernacle
- the geographical locations for the twelve tribes
- the regulations governing the Israelites
- the supernatural presence of the cloud by day and pillar of fire by night
- the supernatural provision of quail
- the opposition of Miriam and Aaron, her disease of leprosy, and her healing as a result of Moses' prayer for her
- the arrival at the borders of Canaan and the exploration of the Promised Land by the twelve spies

As we glance over these circumstances we can see the strong, courageous, capable leadership of Moses during these first few weeks of their trip to the Promised Land. However, the last two events signal the climate of dissension that ultimately led to circumstances resulting in Moses' bout with depression. But signs of trouble are discernible as far back as the supernatural provision of quail from God.

The people rebelled against Moses' leadership, but it wasn't the first time. No, that isn't what caused Moses' depression. Rather, Moses was like the usual person under pressure—He blamed God for his troubles. He considered it an affliction to be under such a load. He thought God had something against him. Some attitude from the man God had entrusted with the leadership of more than three million people!

From that time on, Moses fit the definition of depression. He became self-preoccupied. He lost self-control and self-discipline in his leadership and became more and more depressed.

In his desolate, empty, depressed moments, Moses exclaims: "I cannot carry all these people by myself; the burden is too heavy for me. If this is how you are going to treat me, put me to death right now" (Numbers 11:14–15).

I think we can compare Moses' feelings to our own overworked, underpaid attitudes and discover that we have felt just like Moses. Having felt like him, we've fallen prey to the same bouts of depression.

Have you ever been at a similar point of depression in your life? Describe your feelings:

_____
_____
_____
_____
_____
_____
_____
_____
_____
_____

Let's see how God ministered to Moses.

God gave Moses a guide to lead him through the wilderness. During the forty years that Moses spent in the desert before he assumed the leadership of the Israelites, he married a woman from Midian. He asked his brother-in-law Hobab to travel with them and guide them through the wilderness.

"Moses said to Hobab son of Reuel the Midianite, Moses' father-in-law, 'We are setting out for the place about which the Lord said, "I will give it to you." Come with us and we will treat you well, for the Lord has promised good things to Israel. . . Please do not leave us. You know where we should camp in the desert, and you can be our eyes. If you come with us, we will share with you whatever good things the Lord gives us'" (Numbers 10:29,31).

God gave Moses seventy elders to help him carry the burden of the people. "The Lord said to Moses: 'Bring me seventy of Israel's elders who are known to you as leaders and officials among the people. . . . I will come down and speak with you there, and I will take of the Spirit that is on you and put the Spirit on them. They will help you carry the burden of the people so that you will not have to carry it alone'" (Numbers 11:16–17).

God sent meat for the people to eat. "A wind went out from the Lord and drove quail in from the sea. It brought them down all around the camp to about three feet above the ground, as far as a day's walk in any direction. All that day and night and all the next day the people went out and gathered quail" (Numbers 11:31–32).

The example of Moses indicates to us that we can depend on God to provide guidance, support, and food in our times of depression. The supernatural provision of these three things will shift our attention back to God and away from ourselves and our troubles.

Think back again to your times of depression when you felt like Moses. As you remember such a time, search for the three provisions of God in your circumstances.

How did God provide guidance for you?

What evidence can you see now of God's support of you, either spiritually or materially, through the support of friends, loved ones, and acquaintances?

What was the spiritual food God supernaturally provided in this time?

Elijah: Experiencing God's Intervention

Sometimes one of the most depressing elements in our lives is the recognition of something about us we don't like or we hate to admit is a part of us.

I think we can see this principle at work in the story of Elijah. External circumstances caused this outspoken, courageous man of God to be filled with fear—and this fear paralyzed him, throwing him into the depth of depression.

In 1 Kings 18 and 19 Elijah had just won a monumental victory at Mount Carmel against the prophets of Baal. God had supernaturally revealed himself to Elijah and hundreds of people, burning up the water-soaked altar Elijah had erected. The people recognized the God of Elijah and called out to Him. Then, almost as an afterthought, God sent rain, miraculously ending the drought in the nation.

Look at 1 Kings 18:45–46: "Meanwhile, the sky grew black with clouds, the wind rose, a heavy rain came and Ahab rode off to Jezreel. The power of the Lord came upon Elijah and, tucking his cloak into his belt, he ran ahead of Ahab all the way to Jezreel."

What a testimony to victorious Christian living! I'm sure that as Elijah looks back over this authorized biography of his life from his mansion in heaven, he rejoices over chapter 18. How encouraging to remember times when he charged ahead of troubles in victory!

But chapter 19 experiences await all of us: times when we recognize the frailties within, and our less-than-perfect, carnal responses devastate us and throw us into the depths of depression.

That's what happened to Elijah. This bold, fearless man who stood up to the masses on Mount Carmel now crumples in the face of an individual—the queen.

Read 19:1–4: "Ahab told Jezebel everything Elijah had done and how he had killed all the prophets with the sword. So Jezebel sent a messenger to Elijah to say, 'May the gods deal with me, be it ever so severely, if by this time tomorrow I do not make your life like that of one of them [the dead prophets of Baal].'

"Elijah was afraid and ran for his life. When he came to Beersheba in Judah, he left his servant there, while he himself went a day's journey into the desert. He came to a broom tree, sat down under it and prayed that he might die. 'I have had enough, Lord' he said, 'Take my life; I am no better than my ancestors.' "

Just as significant to this story as the fact that Elijah failed God internally by yielding to his fear is the fact that he failed

God externally by trying to run away from his situation, thus taking himself out of God's direct will.

Elijah traveled eighty days and 480 miles trying to run away from his situation. He was so moved with fear—so depressed and defeated—that he didn't even ask God what to do!

Think about a time in your life when a situation facing you caused you to have a fear reaction and to try to run away from the situation. Briefly recount the incident in your life:

What was the negative internal response that you had to the situation?

What was your external response? Did you try to run away from the situation?

Having recognized your carnal response, and having tried to remove yourself from the situation, did you then experience depression as Elijah did?

Is it possible that you may have prayed that God would end your life as Elijah did?

How did this incident cause you to take yourself out of God's direct will for your life?

One unalterable principle is necessary to recognize at times like this: Eventually we have to come back to the point where we left following the direct will of God in order for God to be able to guide us.

We will see how this principle is at work in the story of Elijah. Let's take a look at how God responded to Elijah.

God met Elijah's physical needs first. "All at once an angel touched him and said, 'Get up and eat.' He looked around, and there by his head was a cake of bread baked over hot coals, and a jar of water. He ate and drank and then lay down again. The angel of the Lord came back a second time and touched him and said, 'Get up and eat, for the journey is too much for you.' So he got up and ate and drank. Strengthened by that food, he traveled forty days and forty nights until he reached Horeb, the mountain of God. There he went into a cave and spent the night" (1 Kings 19:5–8).

God knows that depression has physical and emotional symptoms that need ministering to first. That is the way He responded to Elijah (and we can count on His ministering to us in these areas also).

Notice this important fact: Even though God began to minister to Elijah, Elijah continued to take himself out of God's will. He had already traveled to Beersheba, a distance of about a hundred miles from Jezreel, where he started. From Beersheba he traveled a day's journey into the wilderness, where the angel of the Lord ministered to him.

And yet, after being fed and nourished by the supernatural intervention of God, Elijah still runs another forty days' journey to Mount Horeb.

The interesting thing to me is in the words of the angel. The angel said to Elijah: "Get up and eat, for the journey is too much for you" (v. 7).

The present tense of the verb, *is*, indicates that the angel was talking not about the hundred miles and more that Elijah had already traveled, but Elijah's plan to run even further away.

Even in the times we think God has deserted us, He is with us and knows our fears and plans.

God asked Elijah, "What are you doing here?" God knew that Elijah needed to answer for his actions that had removed him from God's will. Elijah had a well-rehearsed response ready for

God. Two times God asked him what he was doing in that place, and two times Elijah gave the same excuse: "I have been very zealous for the Lord God Almighty. The Israelites have rejected your covenant, broken down your altars, and put your prophets to death with the sword. I am the only one left, and now they are trying to kill me too" (1 Kings 19:10).

One of the characteristics of depression is to have well-rehearsed rationalizations for being depressed. But note how God responds to Elijah. He heard the excuse. He obviously recognized that Elijah had run away from a situation and thus had taken himself out of God's direct will. Yet He was uncondemning and supportive. "Go out and stand on the mountain in the presence of the Lord, for the Lord is about to pass by" (v. 11).

Notice how effectively God was able to take Elijah out of the darkness of his cave experience. A symptom of depression is the feeling that everything has "caved in" upon us and rendered us helpless. Before God even directly ministered to Elijah, He gave him a way out of the darkness and immobility.

God will do the same for us when we struggle with depression. He will put a light beyond the darkness and tell us to move toward that light, because that is where we will meet God, our Source.

Then as Elijah moved outside the cave, God presented some interesting phenomena (to put it mildly). Catch the picture in verses 11 and 12: "Then a great and powerful wind tore the mountains apart and shattered the rocks before the Lord, but the Lord was not in the wind. After the wind there was an earthquake, but the Lord was not in the earthquake. After the earthquake came a fire, but the Lord was not in the fire. And after the fire came a gentle whisper."

What an awesome encounter. I can imagine that God spoke without words to Elijah something like this: "So, Elijah, you feel as though your problems have blown and shattered you into little pieces. Then those little pieces have been scattered by a rumbling from deep within before they could be reassembled. And to complete your devastation you feel as though a raging fire has consumed those scattered pieces, forever destroying the possibility of restoration. Well, Elijah, *here I am!* In the stillness of your devastation, the paralysis of your immobilized emotions, here I am!"

Have you felt like Elijah? Have the winds of your impossible situations blown you apart? Have the shakings and fires of devastation left you immobilized and depressed? Describe the feelings you have:

At the center of your devastation have you heard the gentle whisper of God saying, "Here I am!" How did the recognition of God's presence in your darkest moments make you feel?

But God's intervention in Elijah's depression did not end with that gentle whisper. As Elijah recognized the presence of God he was confronted with that question again: "What are you doing here?"

God won't allow us to cop out and refuse to shoulder the responsibility for our depressions. He gently and firmly causes us to recognize that we have left His will, and that while He met us in the darkness of our wayside cave away from His will, He is there to take us back to the center of His direct will for our lives.

God's instructions to Elijah will be His instructions to us:

"The Lord said to him, 'Go back the way you came' " (1 Kings 19:15).

God gave Elijah a job to do. There is an irony in the job that God gave to Elijah. Remember Elijah's complaint? "I am the only one left, and now they are trying to kill me too."

By these next verses, we can tell that the depression Elijah was experiencing had lifted and flown away. At an earlier point Elijah feared his life was over, about to be destroyed by his enemies. His ministry was coming to an end. No one was left to carry on.

Do you know the job that God gave to Elijah? It was to appoint his successor! That would have devastated him during his depression, and yet here we see him eagerly respond to God's instructions and travel back the 480 miles to carry them out: "So Elijah went from there and found Elisha son of Shaphat. . . . Elijah went up to him and threw his cloak around him" (1 Kings 19:19).

What a transformed attitude we see in Elijah. Expect the same in yourself!

Jonah: Trusting God's Ways

The example of Jonah's depression is not as encouraging as that of Elijah's. Here we never really see the transformation, and yet we recognize the hand of God in dealing with Jonah.

The story begins in the earlier three chapters of the Book of Jonah. God had given Jonah a job to do that he didn't want to do. But a "great fish" convinced him he'd better do it.

So Jonah traveled to Nineveh and forecast destruction unless the people turned to God. Let's pick the story up in Jonah 3: "Jonah obeyed the word of the Lord and went to Nineveh. . . . He proclaimed: 'Forty more days and Nineveh will be overturned.' The Ninevites believed God. . . . When God saw what they did and how they turned from their evil ways, he had compassion and did not bring upon them the destruction he had threatened" (3:3–5,10, KJV).

Hallelujah! The people responded to Jonah's message! How overjoyed and victorious he must have felt!

"*Jonah was greatly displeased and became angry!* He prayed to the Lord, 'O Lord, is this not what I said when I was still at home? That is why I was so quick to flee to Tarshish. I knew that you are a gracious and compassionate God, slow to anger and abounding in love, a God who relents from sending calamity. Now, O Lord, take away my life, for it is better for me to die than to live' " (4:1–3, emphasis added).

Jonah was so angry and depressed at the saving of 120,000 people from death and destruction—*his own converts*—so angry at the goodness of God, that he prayed to die.

Jonah's example reminds us of the many times our depressions are just as unreasonable, illogical, and selfish.

God ministered to Jonah in the midst of his depression:

"Jonah went out and sat down at a place east of the city. There he made himself a shelter, sat in its shade and waited to see what would happen to the city. Then the Lord God provided a vine and made it grow up over Jonah to give shade for his head to ease his discomfort, and Jonah was very happy about the vine. But at dawn the next day God provided a worm, which chewed the vine so that it withered. When the sun rose, God provided a scorching east wind, and the sun blazed on Jonah's head so that he grew faint. He wanted to die, and said, 'It would be better for me to die than to live'" (4:5–8).

The message in God's manner of ministering to Jonah may seem unclear—just as it often is with us in the midst of our depressions, for many times we do not recognize or understand the method of God's ministrations to us.

But I believe that God wanted Jonah to understand that God could not effectively minister to him until Jonah recognized the anger and bitterness within himself. He thought the problem was with the Ninevites—he didn't recognize that it was within himself.

Thus he couldn't understand God's message: "God said to Jonah, 'Do you have a right to be angry about the vine?' 'I do,' he said. . . . 'You have been concerned about this vine, though you did not tend it or make it grow. It sprang up overnight and died overnight. But Nineveh has more than a hundred and twenty thousand people who cannot tell their right hand from their left'" (4:9–11).

That's where the story ends. We have no record to indicate that Jonah ever overcame his depression. But the story leaves an impression we dare not ignore. *Beware the problem within!*

Think about your depression. Has it been long-standing? Have attempts to turn to God for relief seemed to fail? Do you have difficulty recognizing and understanding what God is doing . . . or whether He's doing anything at all?

Perhaps you haven't recognized the problem within! Is there bitterness and anger feeding your depression? What else may be lurking in the darkness of your depression?

Is there a problem within?

When the problem is removed, God can minister to our depression, and His gentle touch will alleviate the darkness and restore us to His direct will for our lives.

Then our testimony will be like David's in Psalm 27:1–3,13–14:

> The Lord is my light and my salvation—whom shall I fear? The Lord is the stronghold of my life—of whom shall I be afraid? When evil men advance against me to devour my flesh, when my enemies and my foes attack me, they will stumble and fall. Though an army besiege me, my heart will not fear; though war break out against me, even then will I be confident. . . . I am still confident of this: I will see the goodness of the Lord in the land of the living. Wait for the Lord; be strong and take heart and wait for the Lord.

3

Rejecting Rejection and Accepting Acceptance

Chapter Focus

Rejection is a feeling that all of us have experienced. But rejection need not destroy or impair our living up to the potential we have in God.

What God's Word Says

"To the praise of the glory of his grace, by which *he has made us accepted* in the Beloved" (Ephesians 1:6, NKJV, emphasis added).

Vignette

When my husband had come to the end of his rope, living life to please himself, addicted to drugs, but now desperately crying out for help, he found himself at a Teen Challenge center. Through the years of rejection and pain, Jim had built walls of protection around himself that made it nearly impossible for others to get close to him. He tells of the kindness of a woman that helped him to begin to lower the walls and receive the love of others:

> A little lady named Irene walked up to me. With her kind face beneath graying hair, she reminded me so much of Mom. She had one arm behind her back, and she smiled at me.

"Hi, Jim," she said, "I'm pleased to meet you. We're so glad you're here."

Man, I thought, *I can't deal with all of this "nice guy" stuff.* I turned away from her.

She walked around me so that I had to face her smile again. "What do you want from me?" I snapped, "Just leave me alone!"

I watched her face as I spoke, expecting her to back off. That's what everyone else always did.

Instead, tears began to fall down her cheeks. She kept on smiling, though, and she stepped closer to me. She brought her tucked-back arm around in front and held out her hand to me.

I looked down to see what she had. There in her hand was a peanut butter sandwich.

"Take it," she said, "I thought you might be hungry." She thrust it in my hand and patted my arm maternally.

"I'm so glad you came," she repeated. The rest of my walls came tumbling down!

The Rejection of Jesus

•Jesus was rejected by family.

"For even his own brothers did not believe in him" (John 7:5).

•Jesus was rejected by friends.

"All the disciples deserted him and fled" (Matthew 26:56b).

•Jesus was rejected by religious leaders.

"Pilate called together the chief priests, the rulers and the people . . . with one voice they cried out, 'Away with this man! Release Barabbas to us! . . . Crucify him! Crucify him!'" (Luke 23:13,18,21).

•Jesus was rejected by His home town.

"'Isn't this the carpenter? Isn't this Mary's son and the brother of James, Joseph, Judas, and Simon? Aren't his sisters here with us?' And they took offense at him" (Mark 6:3).

In spite of the many times Jesus was rejected during His three short years of ministry on Earth, He wasn't destroyed by that rejection. Luke 4:28–30 helps us discover why He could withstand such rejection.

"All the people in the synagogue were furious when they

heard this. They got up, drove him out of the town, and took him to the brow of the hill on which the town was built, in order to throw him down the cliff. But he walked right through the crowd and went on his way."

Those four little words, "went on his way," tell us three important things about Jesus that allowed Him to withstand the rejection people hurled towards Him.

1. Jesus understood His situation in life. He knew He would not be understood and accepted by everyone. Nevertheless, He had a clear vision of His purpose. Nothing, not even rejection, deterred Him from the Father's divine plan.

2. Jesus had a healthy self-image. He knew the value His Heavenly Father placed on Him. He knew His worth came not from His peers or from His friends, but from His God.

3. Jesus was spiritually healthy. He had a vibrant, strong relationship with His Father-God. He was committed to whatever His Father asked of Him—even if it meant being misunderstood and rejected by the people that surrounded Him.

Think about your life. Have you been misunderstood and rejected by those around you? Have you been able to "go on your way"?

Do you understand your situation in life, not just the cause and effect of your circumstances, but your life purpose? What calling does God have on your life?

Have you developed a healthy self-image? How does your Heavenly Father value you? How has He proved your worth to Him?

How spiritually healthy are you? What is the condition of your relationship to your Father-God? Is that the most important relationship to you? How are you attempting to become closer to God?

The Source of Rejection

We experience rejection from many different sources. For most of us, rejection begins in childhood. Let's look at how it begins to take root in a child.

Many times children don't mean to reject one another, but in their teasing, the root may be formed:

"Why'd you drop the ball, clumsy?"

"That was a dumb thing to do!"

"You'd lose your head if it wasn't screwed on!"

"Man, what a nerd!"

Unfortunately children are not the only ones to make these remarks. Both peers and parents often make hurtful comparisons. Sibling rivalry can be cruel, and peer pressure can devastate a child or adolescent, but how tragic when a child must endure these kinds of statements from a parent.

Often parents make comparisons without meaning to hurt.

"If only you were neater—like your sister!"

"Your brother is a natural athlete—but you are really going to have to work to be a good ball player."

"You may have to study harder than your sister to get grades as good as hers, but you can do it."

I remember this was one area where rejection took root in me. My parents were older when they married. Eight years passed before they had their first child, my sister. My mother was almost past the childbearing years, but they didn't want only one child. I was born twenty months later.

Often my parents would say to me, "We had you to be a playmate to your sister." They meant this in the kindest sense, but it devalued me rather than made me feel important. It didn't help that my sister had to study harder in school than I. Many nights she was allowed to study while I was stuck in the kitchen doing the dinner dishes.

Furthermore, false or unattainable expectations can feed the rejection in a child.

"You should have had all A's."

"You never make your bed (after a one-time memory lapse)."

"You should be doing better than that by now."

Even things such as a father wanting a son and getting a daughter or a mother looking forward to a daughter and getting another son can feed rejection.

44

Since my parents' first child had been a girl, they had anticipated I would be a boy. They even had a boy's name picked out. It took them a day or so to select a girl's name after I was born. They often related this story to me. It didn't do much for my self-image (although I should have been grateful—my name was to have been Rufus Milton, after my grandfather).

Adult rejections continue the growth of rejection in many ways. Among them are

•loss of a mate

•loss of friendships

•rejection of a grown child

•failures and losses of job, home, finances, etc.

•self-inflicted hurts because of having been rejected

When rejection is present within us we tend to reject others.

A tiger was reported to be on the rampage in a remote village area of Asia. For many days, the tiger prowled about, destroyed crops and animals, and even came close to villages to threaten children and people who dared venture out of their huts. The village men banded together to capture the tiger. They hunted for many days before they finally found and killed the beast.

When the men brought the tiger back to one of the villages, the people gathered around to take a closer look. They found a deep wound on one of its paws—oozing with pus and infection. The pain the tiger endured had caused it to inflict pain on all who came in its path.

Think back to your childhood. Can you recall childhood rejections that began to take their toll on you? List some of these rejections and your response to them.

What adult rejections have hurt you?

45

Do you build walls to avoid more rejections? How?

The Danger of an Unhealed Hurt

Remember the story of King Saul and David? When David first came to Saul's palace to live, he was well-liked by Saul. He was given a high position in Saul's government. Saul even wanted David for a son-in-law. But the day came when the people liked David better than Saul:

> When the men were returning home after David had killed the Philistine, the women came out from all the towns of Israel to meet King Saul with singing and dancing, with joyful songs and with tambourines and lutes. As they danced, they sang:
>
> > "Saul has slain his thousands,
> > and David his tens of thousands."
>
> Saul was very angry; this refrain galled him. They have credited David with tens of thousands, he thought, but me with only thousands. What more can he get but the kingdom? *And from that time on Saul kept a jealous eye on David* (1 Sam. 18:6–9, emphasis added).

From then on, David lived in fear of Saul. Rejection drove Saul to search obsessively for David. He wanted to kill David and rid himself of this enemy who had stolen the affection of his people.

How different from Saul's response to rejection was that of Jesus. Though rejected often, He inflicted no hurt or rejection on another. He had no wounds to fester and infect others. He found healing from His wounds and offered that same healing to all.

46

Recall recent rejections that still cause you difficulty. Think about someone who has hurt you very deeply by rejecting you.

Write a letter (which you won't mail) to that person. Share your feelings in the letter. Say what you miss most about the relationship you had with that person. Now tell that person what you appreciate about him or her. Offer your forgiveness to that person.

Dear _____

_____

_____

_____

_____

_____

_____

_____

_____

_____

_____

_____

_____

Save the letter. When you feel rejection surface, take the letter out and read it. Remind yourself that with God's help you have forgiven that person and will inflict no pain on him. Pray daily for that person.

Healing from Rejection

There are things you can do to help promote healing from rejection. All of us will face rejection at one time or another. The way we respond to that rejection is up to us. We can be like the wounded tiger and inflict our pain on others. Or we can respond like Jesus, who refused to let the rejection He suffered become a festering wound, and look for ways to offer healing to those who hurt us.

Recognize that you have been hurt. As with handling any negative emotion, the first step to making a positive adjustment to rejection comes in acknowledging the negative feelings. Acknowledge your pain. Be aware that in the future you will face rejection again. Not everyone is going to like you or want to be your friend.

There are three stages you will pass through as you tear down the walls of rejection and learn to reach out to others without fear.

1. You will reach out and extend your friendship to those you consider safe. These will include people who have known you for years and with whom you feel perfectly safe exposing the real you. It also will include those you are confident will not reject your offer of friendship: the retirees in the nursing home, your invalid neighbor, that person in church who has never been married, the one who cuts your hair—these are "safe" relationships.

2. You will reach out to strangers and people you are not sure will accept you even though you still fear rejection. The walls have tumbled slightly. You are still wary of stepping out and forming relationships because of the risk of rejection. But the possibility of enjoying new relationships is worth the risk of becoming vulnerable and perhaps being rejected.

3. You will reach out to all you meet. Some are going to accept you and be your friend and some aren't. But you are ready to offer your friendship freely and willingly. The walls are completely down and your healing is in effect. You are aware that ultimately not everyone will be your friend, but you can freely offer the hand of friendship to others. If a friendship is possible you will develop it, if it isn't, at least you have been willing to try.

Confess your hurts and clean out your wounds. Recognizing the presence of rejection is the first step to getting rid of it. When our children run to us with their banged-up knees the first thing we do is clean out the dirt. We need also to clean out the dirt of rejection. Putting a Band-Aid over the dirt will not effect healing.

48

Rejection hurts, a lot! Rejection sometimes feels as if we are getting spit at in the face, hit on the head, punched in the stomach, and cut off at the knees all at the same time. Rejection triggers embarrassment, self-reproach, self-doubt, humiliation, fear, loneliness and physical pain. So when you are having a rejection experience, acknowledge the pain and take care of yourself.

Extend forgiveness to those who have rejected you. We do not adequately understand God's great gift of forgiveness. If only we could fully comprehend that when we extend forgiveness we receive healing! Forgiveness diffuses the pain of rejection. It "pulls the splinter out" and applies God's grace to our wounds.

You may want to turn to chapter 7 and learn more about extending forgiveness to those who have inflicted pain on you. Your healing will follow your willingness to forgive.

Place yourself in the presence of Jesus and His acceptance. I have a friend who has a hard time believing anyone could love her. But she knows that that feeling comes from her experience of rejection. "I know that I will never be able to fully love others until I rid myself of the root of rejection. I know that I must learn to love myself before I will be able to love others. So when I get up in the morning and look in the mirror, the first thing I say is 'Jesus loves me!' Then after I am all dressed up, have my hair combed just right and my make-up on perfectly, I look in the mirror again. This time I say, 'I love me too.'"

God's grace is sufficient to help us rebuild our lives after they have been torn by rejection. But we have to decide to come into the presence of Jesus in order for that grace to be effective.

Accept yourself as a person God loves. Pray this prayer: "God, I thank You for loving me as I am. Because You love me, I can love myself."

My husband, Jim, often encourages people to pray these words daily: "Lord, show me myself as You see me. Give me a glimpse of what I can become. Teach me what I need to know in order to become that person."

I remember the advice of a speaker who said, "Don't take life too seriously. You won't get out of it alive anyway!"

Reexamine your relationships. Think about the rejected relationships you have had in the past. What caused the rejection? What did the other person find destructive about the relationship?

Often we can make changes in how we go about building relationships, changes that will remove some of the threat of rejection. We can change our ways of relating so they will be more compatible with other people's ways of relating.

Think of someone you would like to develop a friendship with and write that person's name here:

What prior hurts could hinder your relationship with this person?

To whom do you need to extend forgiveness in order to be healed enough to risk the vulnerability of this developing friendship?

How can you bring this new friendship, along with your hopes and dreams for it, into the presence of Jesus?

Develop a prayer stating your hopes and dreams for this friendship.

What destructive patterns have you recognized in your relationship-building?

What changes have you made in order to be ready for this new friendship?

What steps will you take to pursue this relationship?

Rejection need not hinder you forever. If you will follow the guidelines in this chapter, you will be free to develop many new friendships in your future.

Never forget the relationship which should be of paramount importance in your life—your relationship with God.

Reach out to Him:

Rag Doll

Lord, I come to you like a broken rag doll,
My dress is torn and stained,
My arm is half-hanging on.
My eyes aren't shining and trusting like they once were.
And my expression isn't innocent and transparent anymore.
I'm not the unused, brand-new rag doll I once was.
Yes, my smile is still there,
But not as spontaneous as it once was;
It's a little more forced now,
A bit more tired.
I need to be picked up by you, Lord.
Picked up
held tightly
loved
and reassured.
Reassured that no matter how I look,
Or how dirty and scuffed up and broken I am,
You love me just like when I was brand new.
Would you please hold me, Lord?

—Robin Williams

4

Alone or Lonely?

Chapter Focus

We need to discover some ways to deal with our chronic, gripping bouts with loneliness. This chapter will give some biblical principles for the lonely.

What God's Word Says

"God sets the lonely in families" (Psalm 68:6).

"Never will I leave you; never will I forsake you" (Hebrews 13:5).

"I will be with you always, to the very end of the age" (Matthew 28:20).

Vignette

You have probably already read this on a plaque or poster somewhere, but it vividly describes the love and commitment the Heavenly Father has for us.

Footprints in the Sand

I dreamed that I had died. The Lord and I walked side by side, leaving two sets of footprints in the sand. Ahead in the distance, I could see the pearly gates of heaven. I took one last glance behind me, wanting to remember all the footsteps I had taken through life. Behind me, over the smooth and easy paths of my life's journey, there were two sets of footprints. I asked the Lord this question: "Lord, I believed that you would walk by my side all through my life, during easy times and difficult times. But during the hard journeys, I see only one set of footprints. Why?" The Lord answered, "My child, I was with you all through your travels. But along the most difficult paths, I carried you."

If there is one emotion that everyone experiences at one time or another in life, it is loneliness. Loneliness isn't selective; it disregards one's status, wealth, even the number of friends.

For those who have gone through the break-up of a relationship or the loss of a mate or parent, it can become a plague.

In spite of his popularity, Elvis Presley, "King of Rock and Roll," probably felt its throes himself. One of his hit songs spoke of it in a milder form: lonesomeness.

And it's my guess that many people have sat down in the midst of an attack of loneliness and listened to "Are You Lonesome Tonight?"

A man who had recently lost his entire family was asked if he could define the difference between lonesomeness and loneliness. "Lonesome is when somebody is not there and you know they will be back after awhile. Lonely is when you don't have anybody to be lonesome for."

I've experienced both. I get lonesome when Jim is out of town. I even get lonesome for him at times when he is in town—but too busy to be with me when I think I need him most.

But even that feeling is not the emotionally-gripping, paralyzing feeling of chronic loneliness. Many divorced and separated people cope with it for long periods of time. That is real loneliness. It is a feeling that needs to be dealt with, understood, coped with, and then dispensed with as we learn to move further and further away from the devastation of crisis into the hope of a bright new future in God's plan.

I've felt the chronic pain of loneliness also. One time in particular stands out in my memory—not so much because of the intensity of my emotion, as for the intensity of God's response. Both my parents had recently been diagnosed with terminal illnesses: Mom with inoperable cancer, Dad with coronary heart disease. They lived in Michigan. Jim and I lived in the adjacent state of Illinois. But God was leading us in a move that would take us hundreds of miles from my dying parents.

We traveled to Winter Park, Florida, to conduct a seminar for the church where we now minister. While we were there, the pastor and church board asked us to take the position of pastors to single adults.

The decision we faced threw me into the grip of loneliness. How could I consider leaving my parents at a time like this? How could I move clear across the country when they were both given just months to live? Why did I even consider coming to this seminar when my dad lay in an intensive care unit in a hospital in Michigan? They were all I had. The thought of leaving them for a new ministry in Florida seemed impossible.

Alone in the motel room, I knelt by the bed and sobbed for what seemed hours. Then I crawled back into bed, exhausted by the turmoil in my mind. Suddenly I felt arms around me— actual physical arms holding me and soothing my troubled spirit. I turned to thank Jim for realizing that I needed him, and for returning to the room to be with me—but he wasn't there. No one was! But at that moment I recognized the presence of God. I heard Him whisper, "Be still, my child, I'll take care of both your parents and you too!"

One of my favorite verses in my lonely times has always been Isaiah 43:1–3.

"Fear not, for I have redeemed you; I have summoned you by name; you are mine. When you pass through the waters, I will be with you; and when you pass through the rivers, they will not sweep over you. When you walk through the fire, you will not be burned; the flames will not set you ablaze. For I am the Lord, your God, the Holy One of Israel, your Savior."

What experiences have you had with lonesomeness? What do you do for it?

Now share your deeper, more gripping struggles with loneliness. What causes it for you?

How do you deal with it?

What particular Scripture portions have become handles for you to hang onto during your bouts with loneliness?

Sources in Loneliness

There are three sources to whom we normally turn when we are lonely:

Source One: Spouse

This is a normal, God-instituted plan for lonely people. Genesis 2:18 says, "It is not good for the man to be alone." But where do we turn if our mate has left us or is unwilling to be there for us when needed? Then God has a second source for us.

Source Two: Family

One of the verses with which we began this chapter says it best: "God sets the lonely in families" (Psalm 68:6).

This source is open to anyone experiencing loneliness. It doesn't mean just flesh-and-blood family. God has provided support through the body of Christ (see Romans 12:5). This spiritual family can give the nurturing and caring that even our real families often cannot provide.

Jim and I know this is true. We have few flesh-and-blood family members left, none of whom we are close to either geographically or emotionally. Yet God has blessed us with a spiritual family that cares for us and loves us very much. It is difficult to feel lonely with them around.

But what if our mate is gone—and no family, real or spiritual, seems to be present when we need them most. Then the most important source still is available.

Source Three: God

We simply cannot get away from God. Even in our loneliest moment—our darkest hour—He is there with us! Even when we don't feel His presence, He is there! He is there all the time.

"I am with you always, to the very end of the age" (Matthew 28:20). That's the promise He gives the lonely . . . "always"!

Which of these three sources for lifting loneliness has helped you the most: mate, family, or God?

What special secret can you share to help someone learn to use at least the latter two of these sources?

The Causes of Loneliness

What triggers an attack of loneliness? For the single-again person, loneliness attacks frequently. Many times the severity of the attack hinders us from being aware of its cause. But as we become able to identify causes, we can monitor our thoughts and actions, and learn to avoid the things that trigger the attack.

Damaged Emotions

Damaged emotions can trigger an attack of loneliness. The recurring memories of happier times create a sense of loss. At those times, our emotions, already damaged by the crisis, respond in deep pain to the memories and thus an attack of loneliness begins.

A friend of mine from Chicago comes to mind. Patti had been divorced from her husband for several years when I met her. I learned that he had deserted her and their five children (all under the age of seven).

Yet Patti was a survivor. During the time I knew her I rarely saw her struggle with crippling emotions. She provided as well as she could for her little ones and remained positive about the circumstances of her life.

I remember the Thanksgiving season when I took the makings of a Thanksgiving dinner to her home. As I helped her put away the groceries, I opened the refrigerator door to discover only a jar of mustard! Concerned about her need, I began to question her. She cut me off with "Yes, it's been a bad week financially, but I knew God would come through for us somehow!"

Patti worked with us in our ministry to single parent families. Often she would counsel and advise people going through crises far less devastating than her personal crisis. But Patti knew God was her source and she had learned to let Him handle her difficulties.

One day, seven years after her divorce, Patti came to me in tears: "I don't know what's wrong with me," she said through her tears. "I just can't stop crying. I feel so lonely that I don't know if I can go on any longer."

As we talked, I tried to help Patti discover what had triggered this attack of loneliness. We ruled out cause after cause. Then almost out of the blue, Patti rather matter-of-factly stated: "Well, I did get the news that my former husband remarried last week, but that surely couldn't have been the cause. I haven't seen or heard from him in years."

But it was the cause! As we talked about how she felt when she heard the news, she realized that it had triggered memories of how it used to be. The news had allowed lost dreams of how it might have been to surface. Hopes of how it would be again had awakened within.

We need to be aware of the negative potential of recurring memories. When these memory tapes begin to play in our minds, we must turn them off and concentrate on the new thing God is doing in our lives.

Physical Needs

Divorced people are used to the physical and sexual contact of married life. The sudden break off of this contact can trigger deep loneliness. In fact this loneliness is the very thing that causes many single-again individuals to maintain physical and sexual contact with their former mates long after the emotional and familial bonds have been broken. Naturally this hinders their recovery.

While all single adults will have struggles in the area of sexuality, this will be true especially for the single again. This trigger to loneliness will need to be understood and recognized so the individual can make a positive adjustment in this area.

Additional Responsibilities

The added responsibilities of the suddenly-single-parent may trigger loneliness.

The crisis of divorce brings many changes to the custodial parent. Many people face debts and inadequate finances at this time. Others find themselves thrust into the job market for the first time in years. The home responsibilities increase, and parental responsibility is immense. These added pressures cause the parent to feel alone and isolated.

Loss of Togetherness

The loss of enjoyed togetherness can trigger loneliness.

Even if there was not a vibrant, growing relationship with your former mate in the period before the divorce, it is likely that such times of togetherness were shared earlier. Many former relationships were comfortable, and the absence of this will cause loneliness.

Stigma of Divorce

The stigma of divorce can cause loneliness.

Divorced people often feel this stigma in the religious community. They feel the weight of the label "divorced." Although this label doesn't matter in the secular world, it causes many in the church to be ostracized.

One person put it this way:

Life of a Leper

It's been about a year ago
I got this dread disease.
It's grown into a massive wound
That everyone can see.
The unsaved take no second look
For they're unclean as me.
But many Christians judge and stare
And sigh with sympathy.

The thoughts they think show on their face
Behind a plastic grin.
My well-trained eye perceives they think I'm ill
Because I've sinned.
But—I don't mind, I'm used to this
I know I'll never win.
For who but Christ would open up
And really take me in?

And so, I spend my time alone
Just Jesus Christ and me.
To live a life condemned, unclean,
With pain for company.
But what is worse, I look ahead.
No love I can foresee.
For I've been labeled by the church
The Christian Divorcee.

— John DePaul

Rejection

Rejection can trigger loneliness.

It isn't the first rejection of a former mate alone that causes the problem—it's the repeated rejections by friends, former family members, acquaintances, church members, and married people.

Many of them do not realize that the way they are acting is perceived as rejection by the divorced person. Yet the one who is

59

divorced is no longer asked to participate in couple-related activities, is not invited home for Sunday dinners, can no longer drop in at former family members' homes for coffee, and doesn't fit into the same Sunday school class, fellowship group, or social circle.

Whether it comes from these six causes or others unmentioned, an attack of loneliness can be devastating. The effects pervade the life of the formerly married long after the crisis has taken place.

A California study, taken eighteen months after divorces had been finalized, indicates the recurrence of the problem of loneliness:

> The pervasiveness of profound loneliness among men and women was striking. Two-fifths of the men and two-thirds of the women described themselves as lonely, about half of them painfully so. . . .
>
> Among those men and women dating, but not yet settled into a remarriage or steady relationship, there was a weariness with the superficiality of the social scene and the succession of individuals who had passed through their lives.

Consider your encounter with each of these causes to loneliness. Give a brief description of an occurrence and how you dealt with the attack.

Damaged emotions

Physical needs

Added responsibilities

Loss of togetherness

Stigma of divorce

Rejection

Results of Loneliness

There are three stages an individual generally passes through in responding to an attack of loneliness. These move the individual progressively toward a more positive adjustment to loneliness. Each is a valid response to loneliness. We need, however, to check on ourselves to be sure we are progressing steadily toward stage three.

Stage One: Withdrawal

What is our first response when we become lonely? Isn't it to isolate ourselves from other people because we feel so bad? Yet that is when we need people the most.

Read the account of an attack of loneliness experienced by the prophet Elijah. The entire episode is recorded in 1 Kings 19, but Paul gives us a synopsis in Romans 11:2–5:

"God did not reject his people, whom he foreknew. Don't you know what the Scripture says in the passage about Elijah—how he appealed to God against Israel: 'Lord, they have killed your prophets and torn down your altars; I am the only one left, and they are trying to kill me.' And what was God's answer to him? 'I have reserved for myself seven thousand who have not bowed the knee to Baal.' So too, at the present time there is a remnant chosen by grace."

Elijah withdrew almost five hundred miles from where the attack occurred.

That puts us in pretty good company, doesn't it?

I remember a friend's statement to me in Chicago: "I feel so lonely," she related. "But I don't feel safe among very many people yet. So when I get so lonely that I can't stand it anymore, I do one of two things: Either I bake a pie for the shut-in down the street and go visit her, or I offer to babysit for my neighbor's children. I know both of those things will make me feel less lonely."

Can you recall when you may have responded to an attack of loneliness by withdrawing?

How did you withdraw?

What was the result of your withdrawing?

What "safe" activity did you find to dispel the loneliness?

Stage Two: Busyness

More spring-cleaning is completed during attacks of loneliness than at any other time in a person's life.

Many lonely people try to immerse themselves in isolated activities. Their lives become tight little balls of frenzied activity. This tends to isolate them even further from other individuals who could help dispel the loneliness.

The busyness of stage two is engaged in by the person who feels safe enough to step into the mainstream of life again, but not yet comfortable with quiet times and reflective moments, and so becomes very busy with a myriad of activity.

The Bible admonishes us to "be still, and know that I am God" (Psalm 46:10). Although busyness is a normal response to loneliness, our loneliness cannot be overcome by mere activity.

Have you ever tried to overcome your loneliness with busyness?

What busyness did you involve yourself with?

Did it lead to a permanent lessening of your loneliness?

What were the negative results of your busyness?

The final stage of loneliness is when we learn to turn it into opportunities for solitude.

What a golden opportunity single adults have for moments of solitude. At times my busy schedule makes me yearn for solitude. Often the only time I can be alone is when I lock myself in the bathroom. Even there a voice on the other side of the door may ask, "Mommy, are you almost ready to come out?"

Solitude is quality time. We are forced to depend on God in those moments. We can experience the overflow of His love as we shut the world out and let Him minister to us.

There is a beautiful example of quality solitude in the story of Paul the apostle. After Paul's conversion on the road to Damascus, he spent a long period of time in Tarsus. He waited alone for whatever God had prepared for him. We don't know what Paul did during those long years alone, but we can see what Christ did for Paul during that time.

In the solitude Christ was making Paul into the man of God He had created him to be. His theology changed. He developed from a legalistic Pharisee to liberated saint; from a belief that Jesus of Nazareth was a dangerous traitor to the Jewish nation to the conviction that He was the expected Messiah; from a persecutor of the Church to a builder of the Church.

During that time of aloneness God was getting Paul ready for the world and the world ready for Paul.

We can learn to see our solitude as our preparation for the world. Our Christian character can be shaped, as was Paul's, until with him we proclaim:

"For to me, to live is Christ" (Philippians 1:21).

"I resolved to know nothing while I was with you except Jesus Christ and him crucified" (1 Corinthians 2:2).

What a marvelous time of preparation this was for Paul. What a marvelous preparation our alone times can be for us. Read about the revelation of Christ and His character that Paul developed during his preparation time.

"Praise be to the God and Father of our Lord Jesus Christ, who has blessed us in the heavenly realms with every spiritual blessing in Christ. For He chose us in him before the creation of the world to be holy and blameless in his sight. In love he predestined us to be adopted as his sons through Jesus Christ, in accordance with his pleasure and will—to the praise of his glorious grace, which he has freely given us in the One he loves. In him we have the redemption through his blood, the forgiveness of sins in accordance with the riches of God's grace that he lavished on us with all wisdom and understanding. And he made known the mystery of his will according to his good pleasure, which he purposed in Christ to be put into effect when the times will have reached their fulfillment—to bring all things in heaven and on earth together under one head, even Christ" (Ephesians 1:3-10).

"In him we were also chosen, having been predestined according to the plan of him who works out everything in conformity with the purpose of his will, in order that we, who were the first to hope in Christ, might be for the praise of his Glory. And you also were included in Christ when you heard the word of truth, the gospel of your salvation. Having believed, you were marked in him with a seal, the promised Holy Spirit, who is a deposit guaranteeing our inheritance until the redemption of those who are God's possession—to the praise of his glory" (Ephesians 1:11-14).

Have you ever wondered how Paul, a good Jewish boy educated by the leading Jewish professor of that day, Gamaliel, could enter into ministry with such a clear and well-developed Christian theology?

He didn't get it sitting at the feet of Gamaliel—he got it learning at the feet of Christ during those years of solitude in Tarsus! The years of preparation made him ready, just as our alone times can prepare us to be ready to be the person God created us to be.

Have you entered stage three of your loneliness and utilized solitude as a time of preparation?

What has God taught you through your solitude?

The Cure for Loneliness

There are three steps that we can take that will cure our loneliness.

Step One: Learn to Face Circumstances

I've become used to the nonanswers single adults give me when I ask them, "How are you this week?" So many singles try to hide from the realities of their new, single-again situations. They are lonely, frustrated, confused, and in great pain. With tears (or mascara) running down their faces they reply to a "How are you?" with "Oh, I'm just fine."

That's surrender, yielding to the negative power of loneliness. Facing our situations and learning to make the necessary adjustments de-emphasizes the negative power of loneliness, causing it to lose its power and control over us. That was my husband's experience:

> I hadn't been in the ministry long before something else began to happen. I had never in my Christian life felt different than anyone else because of my past. I had never suffered from rejection or the stigma of divorce until I became a minister.
>
> But as I attended ministers' meetings, I experienced some rejection. There were usually three sign-in sheets at these meetings: one for 'ordained pastors,' another for 'licensed pastors,' and a third that read 'others.' Many times, while the rest of the pastors lined up at the first two lists, I walked alone over to the 'others.'
>
> My heart ached. I didn't feel like some fly-by-night preacher. I felt anointed and blessed by God to do what I was doing. Yet when meeting organizers asked for new ministers in the area to stand, I couldn't stand. It was humiliating for me at the time.

Yet God ministered to Jim in his aloneness, and the day came when he was able to say:

> Suddenly the issue was no longer important to me! I had been looking for acceptance in a piece of paper, yet God had already provided that acceptance, unconditionally, in the hearts of His servants. I was totally accepted, totally loved. And a piece of paper could never make me feel more accepted or loved. The

rejection and stigma I had felt had been in my own mind. Once I let go of that rejection, it was gone.

What are the realities of your situation which you have learned, or need to learn, to accept?

Step Two: Learn to Accept Healing

There is a quality of healing in loneliness. Loneliness allows us the time to reflect and visualize new possibilities, new growth. It lets us learn independence—not from people, but from the crutches of our past.

Step Three: Learn to Develop New Relationships

A later chapter will deal in-depth with learning the steps to building good relationships.

One of the key elements to a good relationship is vulnerability. Yet for the single-again individual this is a very difficult issue. Perhaps this verse in Luke 6:38 will help.

"Give and it will be given to you. A good measure, pressed down, shaken together and running over, will be poured into your lap. For with the measure you use, it will be measured to you."

So many times we associate that verse with the material, tangible parts of our life. But it is rich in meaning for relationship building also.

Read the Dycus paraphrase:

"Give yourself to others and they will give themselves back to you, in good measure, squeezed in close around you, bunched together by mutual love and running over with fellowship and support. These relationships will be poured out upon your life. For with the measure of yourself that you give to others, they will give of themselves back in love to you."

What are the ways that you can facilitate such friendships?

List the names of friends and acquaintances with whom you will become more vulnerable so you might develop better relationships.

Now list some of your strategies for accomplishing this.

God loves you! Nothing will ever separate you from God's love. Believing this will help you in walking through the loneliness stimulated by memories, rejection, stigma, and overburdened responsibilities.

It will help you because you have someone constantly holding your hand and walking with you.

"Never will I leave you; never will I forsake you" (Hebrews 13:5).

5

Handling Emotional Stress

Chapter Focus

You can cope more positively with the stress in your life and use it to become a stronger and better individual.

What God's Word Says

"Consider it pure joy, my brothers [and sisters], whenever you face trials [crises] of many kinds, because you know that the testing of your faith [through stress] develops perseverance. Perseverance must finish its work so that you may be mature and complete, not lacking anything" (James 1:2–4).

"Being confident of this, that he who began a good work in you will carry it on to completion until the day of Christ Jesus" (Philippians 1:6).

Vignette

When our eldest child was three years old, he was diagnosed with a speech impairment. We began speech therapy. His difficulty was with substituted and distorted sounds. The speech therapist explained that this part of the brain could be developed with sequencing exercises. She recommended that we purchase a computerized toy for him to use called "Simon."

As I watched Jimmy becoming more and more proficient with

Simon, I decided anyone could do it. In fact, I assumed I would be able to do it at its most difficult level with no sweat.

One night I played the game. Over and over I tried to answer its color-coded responses in proper sequence. Again and again Simon blurted out its rude "Bla-a-chh!" at me as I failed. I became intensely challenged by the game. I heard the sequence, memorized it quickly, and then intently struggled to repeat the sequence back to Simon. By then I was so annoyed and frustrated with the thing that I continued to miss the sequence. Finally I threw it down and muttered to myself, "Dumb game!"

Later, as I calmly thought back over my attempt (and failure) at Simon, I recognized the problem. The rationality of my knowledge of the proper sequence was short-circuited by the irrationality of my emotions.

Just as the emotional response I was making to Simon caused me to handle stress poorly, so the emotional responses we often make to life's "Simon situations" may cause us to be so stressed out that we cannot calmly and rationally use the knowledge we have that could move us into recovery.

Think over your crisis of divorce. Using the two columns below, first list the knowledge you have gained, which should aid your crisis recovery. Then decide what emotion (if any) is short-circuiting your using that knowledge to move toward recovery.

Knowledge Gained   Your Short-
About Crisis   Circuited Emotions

Do you believe that you have more than the normal amount of stress in your life?

Would you say that this stress has made a positive or negative contribution to your emotional and physical life?

_____Positive
_____Negative

If you've attended a divorce recovery seminar or completed the beginning of this book or read any book about crisis and recovery, no doubt you have recognized that the confusion and upheaval from your crisis somehow fits a pattern.

If there is one thing that can be said about a crisis's confusion—its emotional highs and lows, its traumatic changes—it is that such feelings and emotions are normal. Yet many continue to ask themselves, "I wonder why I still feel this way?"

As we begin to develop a perspective on the stress in our lives, let's clarify what we mean by the term: Stress is any chronically present life situation that constantly irritates (including worried anticipation of the future and preoccupation with the past). Is it any wonder that the experience of divorce is nationally recognized as one of the greatest contributors to stress?

Complete the following definitive work sheet about your "life situation":

What life situation is causing you the greatest stress?

How is this situation "chronically present"?

How does this situation "constantly irritate"?

How has this life situation caused you to have a "worried anticipation of the future"?

How has it caused you to be "preoccupied with the past"?

In his book *Marital Separation,* Dr. Robert Weiss describes what he calls "separation distress." He says it is a focusing of attention on the lost person (preoccupation with the past) together with intense discomfort because of that person's inaccessibility (worried over the future).

It is this separation distress that causes short-circuited emotions in our divorce recovery.

Jim and I had a friend in Chicago who had lost a leg during the Korean War. Many times he would say to us, "My leg is killing me today!" I used to think that was a strange comment. Then I learned about the medical phenomenon for such pain—"phantom limb distress." Even though he had no leg, his nervous system was acting as though the limb was still attached.

Although we no longer have a mate, we may often feel this way—which naturally leads to much stress during our recovery period.

It is also natural to assume that life would be better without stress. Yet some stress is actually needed for us to live well-adjusted lives.

How about the stress of that wonderfully inventive snooze alarm in the morning? Don't you set it early on purpose so you can turn it off several times?

Or how about trying to leave for work on time? No matter how early you rise in the morning, do you often end up rushing during those last ten minutes before it's time to leave?

How about household chores? Isn't it more fulfilling to be doing three or four of them at the same time?

What about the garbage? Don't you wait to take it out until you hear the roar of the garbage truck down the street? My husband's secretary does. One day she was busy in her second floor office at our church in Chicago when she heard the familiar roar of the garbage truck arriving in the alley below her office window. She suddenly became aware of the over-flowing wastebasket in her office. Knowing it was Friday, she hurried down the steps, flung open the alley door, called frantically to the garbage man already two doors away, "Wait a minute . . . am I too late?" Without a hint of stress himself, he called right back, "No, hop right on!"

Rather than trying to eliminate all sources of stress, we need to develop a perspective that enables us to cope with both the necessary and unnecessary stresses in our lives.

Stress in a Crisis

Since divorce is a crisis, let's begin by taking a closer look at the characteristics of a crisis. We want to be aware that a crisis such as divorce brings characteristic symptoms.

A crisis is temporary and will not always remain with us.

Our thinking and reasoning abilities are affected by a crisis.

A crisis causes psychosomatic or physical illnesses at times.

Normal ways of handling problems don't seem to apply to a crisis.

A crisis causes a paralysis of thought or will. ("I know I shouldn't be dwelling on this, but I just can't help it." "I know it's too soon for another relationship, but I need somebody so much right now.")

A crisis causes us to use exaggerated defense mechanisms, such as building emotional walls or resorting to repressed or regressive emotions.

Fear or panic often results from a crisis.

How do we begin recognizing the things that are causing us stress? Oh, I know, it's hard to miss the fourteen kids or the fourteen hundred bills due at the end of the month, but what about little daily irritations? Some of the following list may apply to your situation, some may not, but they all can contribute to the stress levels of life.

- Boredom
- Time schedules
- Excessive workload (which can be caused by external sources such as demands of single parenting. It can also be caused by internal sources, such as a frenzied, frantic drive to prove, "I can do it!")
- Role conflicts
- Job insecurity
- Finances (particularly lack of finances)
- Closed, or paralyzed, emotions or communication
- Self-esteem built on a faulty or inadequate base (such as "I am what I do")
- Misunderstanding of normal developmental stages

Can you name any additional stressors in your life?

Developing a Biblical Perspective About Stress

Simply identifying the things that cause stress in our lives won't make them go away. Neither will recognizing the negative way we have been trying to deal with them. Diagnosis of an illness is good, but treatment is what makes the difference.

Look again at the verses of Scripture that opened the chapter:

"Consider it pure joy, my brothers [and sisters], whenever you face trials [crises] of many kinds, because you know that the testing of your faith [through stress] develops perseverance. Perseverance must finish its work so that you may be mature and complete, not lacking anything" (James 1:2–4).

"Being confident of this, that he who began a good work in you will carry it on to completion until the day of Christ Jesus" (Philippians 1:6).

These portions of Scripture are some of those "come on, let's get real" gems, aren't they? They're easy to understand, but . . .

The Dycus paraphrase of the verses in James would go something like this:

"Hey, folks, laugh about that crisis. If you don't laugh—you're going to cry anyway. That crisis is guaranteed to cause you a lot of stress and that stress is going to prove what you are made of. If you have enough stick-to-itiveness you will use that crisis to turn you into what you're meant to be. You will be better than you were before the crisis happened."

I have seen this take place in the lives of divorced people over and over again. The very life situation that at one point threatened to do them in becomes the catalyst that turns those weaklings into some of the strongest people anywhere, able to accomplish great things for God.

We need to get ourselves in a place where handling the difficulties is possible through the Lord's help and through His perspective.

Recognizing the Symptoms of Stress

Let's develop a personal perspective for dealing with stress based on biblical principles.

Psalm 35 is a beautiful example of King David's recognition of the situation facing him, and the stress he was having because of it. Read his analysis of the situation.

"Contend, O Lord, with those who contend with me; fight against those who fight against me. Take up shield and buckler; arise and come to my aid. Brandish spear and javelin against those who pursue me. Say to my soul, 'I am your salvation.' May those who seek my life be disgraced and put to shame; may those who plot my ruin be turned back in dismay. May they be like chaff before the wind, with the angel of the Lord driving them away; may their path be dark and slippery, with the angel of the Lord pursuing them" (vv. 1–6).

We have to be able to identify the enemy in order to persevere in battle. Otherwise those short-circuited emotions drain off our power and we can't move ahead with our recovery.

Some of the symptoms of short-circuited emotions at the onset of stress are listed below:

•Apprehension, anxiety, or panic

•Tension, loss (or gain) of sleep or appetite

- Loss of attention
- Deep sadness, regret for lost happiness
- Loss of self-worth
- Temporary euphoria or denial

Do any of these short-circuited emotions give you trouble?

Moving Forward through Stress

Crises and stress are—without a doubt—valley experiences. But when in the valley, you must go through the valley! Don't stand still.

That's what perseverance is all about. Remember the story of the little engine that could? The little train engine made it all the way to the top of the hill by continually affirming to itself: "I think I can . . . I think I can . . . I think I can!" And it could!

King David recognized this principle in Psalm 35. Read his response.

"My soul will rejoice in the Lord and delight in his salvation. My whole being will exclaim, 'Who is like you, O Lord? You rescue the poor from those too strong for them, the poor and needy from those who rob them' " (vv. 9–10).

Look for that light at the end of the tunnel and aim straight for it. Don't quit until you get there.

Where are you on your journey through your valley?

> What areas in your life need fresh determination and perseverance in order to leave the valley of stress behind?

Accepting Your New Life Willingly

Read how King David felt as he recognized the end of his valley experiences.

"Wait for the Lord and keep his way. He will exalt you to inherit the land; when the wicked are cut off, you will see it. . . . Consider the blameless, observe the upright; there is a future for the man of peace. . . . The salvation of the righteous comes from the Lord; he is their stronghold in time of trouble. The Lord helps them and delivers them; he delivers them from the wicked and saves them, because they take refuge in him" (Psalm 37:34,37,39–40).

How do we recognize the end of our valley experience? We discover the light is in front of us and the darkness is behind us. We learn to believe that the best is yet to come. (Read Jeremiah 29:11.)

"See I have placed before you an open door that no one can shut" (Revelation 3:8).

"Being confident of this, that he who began a good work in you will carry it on to completion until the day of Christ Jesus" (Philippians 1:6).

I've always liked the Achiever's Creed:

> "Whatever the mind can conceive
> and I will dare to believe,
> With God's help, I can achieve."

As we develop that biblical perspective on stress in our lives, the joy will begin to overtake us. Joy has nothing at all to do with our circumstances, but it has everything to do with our response to our circumstances.

78

Adopt the perspective that will help you survive the stresses of your crisis:

I recognize the symptoms of stress in my life.

I commit myself to continual perseverance in order to move forward out of my short-circuited response to stress.

I willingly and joyfully accept the new life that is mine as I come out of my valley experience.

Without a biblical perspective we will never experience pure joy. Remember the woman at the well of Samaria (John 4). Her broken life was filled with stress. Her coping skills were inadequate. She was projecting her stress—placing her guilt on her husbands and lovers. Her reality was completely gone. Then she met Christ and adopted His biblical perspective on the stress in her life.

She made it through the valley. She did it with great joy. And she went on to start the first divorce recovery program in history right there in her own town.

She achieved her dream. And so can you!

6

Sexuality and the Single Again

Chapter Focus

There is no off button to help us cope with our sexuality after we have become single again. We must seek understanding, compassion, and encouragement to face this readjustment to single life. One place we will find such help is in the Bible.

What God's Word Says

"The night is nearly over; the day is almost here. So let us put aside the deeds of darkness and put on the armor of light. Let us behave decently, as in the daytime, not in orgies and drunkenness, not in sexual immorality and debauchery, not in dissension and jealousy. Rather, clothe yourselves with the Lord Jesus Christ, and do not think about how to gratify the desires of the sinful nature" (Romans 13:12–14).

Vignette

Jim and I have a friend named Jack whose wife had taken their children and moved far away. We went with Jack to find an apartment. We fixed him up with some furniture and several frozen homecooked meals. Several weeks later we asked him how he was doing.

"Oh, Pastor Jim, not too good," Jack replied, "I just can't sleep at night." Upon further probing we discovered that he never had gone into the bedroom of his apartment to sleep at night. He slept in a reclining chair in the living room. When we asked him why he did this he replied, "I just can't bring myself to crawl into that bed all alone."

Being a quick thinker, Jim came up with a solution to Jack's problems. He went to the Salvation Army store and purchased the biggest teddy bear he could find. Then he put it in a dress and took it over to Jack's apartment. He placed it in Jack's bed with this note: "Now you can get a good night's rest."

Although Jim's solution provided a lot of humor, it was of little help!

We are a new creation if Jesus has become the Lord and Savior of our lives. The guilt for past sin has been eradicated from our lives. God has put His Spirit within us, and we have the power we need to grow to our full potential in Christ.

Yet if you are single again, the issue of Christian sexuality can be a hot topic. After all, you have legitimately learned to express sexual passion in sexual activity that has ceased; now those passions will be a source of temptation again in your experience as a Christian single.

The expression of sexuality within marriage is a gift from God. Those who have experienced the reality of that gift will miss it when it has been removed from them.

Genesis 2:18–24 gives us God's view of sexuality.

The Lord God said, "It is not good for man to be alone. I will make a helper [appropriate partner] suitable for him.'

Now the Lord God had formed out of the ground all the beasts of the field and all the birds of the air. He brought them to the man to see what he would name them; and whatever the man called each living creature, that was its name. So the man gave names to all the livestock, the birds of the air and all the beasts of the field.

But for Adam no suitable helper was found. So the Lord God caused the man to fall into a deep sleep; and while he was sleeping, he took one of the man's ribs and closed up the place with flesh. Then the Lord God made a woman from the rib he had taken out of the man and he brought her to the man.

The man said, "This is now bone of my bones and flesh of my flesh; she shall be called woman, for she was taken out of man.'

> For this reason a man will leave his father and mother and be
> united to his wife, and they will become one flesh.

God instituted marriage. Yet since 1975, the Department of Health and Human Services has reported that more than a million people a year get a divorce.

In the issue of sexuality it is impossible to find any reasonable or rational source of help from the world today. The gap between the world's view of sexuality and God's view of sexuality is wider than between any other topic.

For a time it seemed as though there was nothing that could slow down the spread of sexual immorality in our world. It's sad that only venereal disease and the advent of AIDS has had any lasting effect on sexual immorality. But the principles guiding the world in its view of "safe sex" are as immoral as the rampant sexual activity that preceded them.

Morton Hunt, Christian psychologist and author, has stated:

"It [sex] becomes either a painkiller that gives temporary relief from a sense of failure or personal undesirability, or a mood elevator that counteracts chronically low self-esteem . . . they get no satisfaction after all; they feel good about themselves, reassured, for a short time after each 'fix,' but within a day or two, or even within hours, the buoyant mood dissipates and anxiety, despair, and self-contempt creep back in."

It is an obvious minority of Christian singles who understand that sex is a gift from God, with great responsibilities, that should be reserved for the marital relationship.

Not only does the world fail to offer answers for the once-married single person struggling with postmarital sexual expression, but the church has been silent as well.

What is the solution to this issue of sexuality? We can begin to answer that question by looking at Jesus' words.

"I have come that they may have life [even after divorce], and have it to the full" (John 10:10).

Many single again persons feel that what they have "to the full" are problems and anxieties and unmet needs.

Discover that the answer to the issue of sexuality lies not in getting rid of your sexual feelings, but in learning to apply spiritual principles to your sexuality. First, realize that Jesus understands your frustrations with your sexuality.

Listen to the words of Hebrews 4:15: "We do not have a high priest who is unable to sympathize with our weaknesses, but we have one [Jesus] who has been tempted in every way, just as we are—yet was without sin."

Hebrews 2:17–18 says: "[Jesus] had to be made like his brothers in every way, in order that he might become a merciful and faithful high priest in service to God, and that he might make atonement for the sins of the people. Because he himself suffered when he was tempted, he is able to help those who are being tempted."

Although He never sinned, Jesus experienced every kind of temptation while He lived on earth. He understands every moment of temptation we face, and stands ready to help us overcome and be victorious every time.

But what if we don't overcome? What if we aren't victorious?

"My dear children, I write this to you so that you will not sin. But if anybody does sin, we have one who speaks to the Father in our defense—Jesus Christ, the Righteous One" (1 John 2:1).

(Don't you love the little "buts" and "ifs" of God's Word?)

What encouragement have you received from non-Christian friends and relatives that has helped you maintain purity as a single again?

What encouragement have you received from Christian friends and relatives that has helped you maintain purity as a single again?

Write down the portions of Scripture that have been a source of encouragement to you.

Using the Escape Route

The accuser, Satan, loves to torment us about our sexuality. He uses lines like these: "If you really were a Christian . . . ," and "If only you had . . . or hadn't . . ."

The combination of loneliness, rejection, and guilt provides Satan with endless opportunities for accusations. He attempts to undermine our resolve to be pure as a Christian single with this accusation: "If you really were a Christian single following God's pattern for sexual purity, you wouldn't have these needs!"

How do we find an escape route to avoid the failure caused by Satan's accusations and toward the victory that awaits us in Christ Jesus?

There are three steps we must follow:

1. When we encounter sexual temptation we must immediately look for a way out. The Bible clearly says it's there: "No temptation has seized you except what is common to man. And God is faithful; he will not let you be tempted beyond what you can bear. But when you are tempted, he will also provide a way out so that you can stand up under it" (1 Corinthians 10:13).

2. When we find that way out, we must use it! Many times when Satan tempts us we look over at the escape route and say, "Oh well, I'll wait a while longer—I can always get to the escape in time."

We need to act like Christian thoroughbreds, straining at the gate, waiting to charge through to victory. The moment we find God's way out we must use it.

First Corinthians 6:18–20 gives us some sound advice: "Flee from sexual immorality. All other sins a man commits are outside his body, but he who sins sexually sins against his own body. Do you not know that your body is a temple of the Holy Spirit, who is in you, whom you have received from God? You are not your own; you were bought at a price. Therefore honor God with your body."

3. Trust God to help you resist temptations. A beautiful promise is given in 2 Peter 2:9: "The Lord knoweth how to deliver the godly out of temptation."

We can trust God to help us with our struggle for sexual purity. We don't have to be embarrassed to ask His help in this area of our lives. He stands ready to rescue us and lead us to spiritual victory.

Have you learned to look immediately for a way out when you find yourself struggling sexually?

What are some of the methods that God has used to help you find it?

How has He helped you understand the value of immediate escape?

Briefly explain some of the ways you have learned to trust God to help you be victorious in your Christian sexuality.

Using Wisdom

Nothing the world has taught us about dating and relationships with the opposite sex is useful in building Christian relationships. The very concept of dating was dreamed up by the world. We need to learn a whole new way of monitoring our fellowship and social situations with the opposite sex.

Determine to avoid putting yourself into a compromising situation with the opposite sex.

Being in a situation where you and a person of the opposite sex are alone for large chunks of time is a compromising situation. You may discover that dating is a compromise. It may be better for you to opt for times of fellowship with that person where you can remain in the company of other Christian brothers and sisters.

It is important for you to decide what becomes a compromising situation for you and your special friend.

If some situation is completely harmless for you but is a compromising situation for your friend, respect your friend's level of non-compromise.

I remember when Jim and I began dating. I had been raised with deeply ingrained biblical principles regarding my sexuality. I had maintained my purity and had not compromised in isolated one-on-one dating situations. But it was different for Jim.

Listen to his description of his feelings.

> What did I know about dating a pure girl? Barb was the first woman I'd been with since years before. I hadn't cared about women much during my last years as an addict, and I had hardly even looked at them since my conversion. I didn't much want to be around them. To me they represented flesh and failure. I had never had a good, fulfilling relationship with any woman—let alone a Christian woman. I kept them at a distance, always giving myself space to walk away to ward off being hurt. But Barb was already inside those walls, and I wanted to keep her there. Yet what did I know about establishing a godly relationship with her?
>
> I knew my limitations. My policy was strictly 'Look but do not touch.' I didn't even shake her hand! My lack of expression confused her. Even though I was feeling many emotions that I hadn't experienced in years, and some that I'd never experienced, telling her about them was still too hard for me to do. I hadn't told her of my limitations, so she didn't know what the problem was.

Communication before the problem of compromise appears is vital! Establish lines of communication early in your relationship with your special friend.

Determine to avoid overexposure.

A beautiful illustration of this is the story of Joseph in the household of Potiphar (Genesis 39:1–12).

Joseph had become a trusted aide to Potiphar, the captain of the king's guard. He was given authority over Potiphar's entire household.

The Bible says Joseph was "well-built and handsome"—a hunk. This was not lost on Potiphar's wife, because "after a while" she approached him directly: "'Come to bed with me!'" Joseph refused, but that did not put a stop to it. This woman approached Joseph "day after day" (v. 10). Whenever her huband was gone, she would invite Joseph to her bed.

At the beginning of this temptation, Joseph tried to give a reasoned response by talking to her about what a great breach of her husband's trust it would be, and "'How . . . could I do such a wicked thing and sin against God?'" (v. 9). After that, he tried to stay as far away from her as possible, apparently hoping the situation would cool down.

But it didn't. One day when she found Joseph alone in the house, she grabbed him by his coat and demanded that he make love to her. This time Joseph didn't try to reason with her. (Perhaps he was, at this point, the inspiration for Paul's advice to Timothy, "Flee . . . youthful lusts" [2 Timothy 2:2, KJV].) Not bothering to save his coat, Joseph shrugged it off and got out of there as fast as he could.

He didn't risk overexposure to the situation. Can you imagine what might have been the outcome of the story if he had said, "Oh, Mrs. Potiphar, perhaps we can just sit down and talk this over"!

Determine to avoid activities that overstimulate you sexually.

Jim didn't even hold my hand for many dates. I had to grab his hand on our eleventh date as we walked through Chicago's Museum of Science and Industry! By that time I was feeling a little like one of the petrified exhibits in the museum.

I remember the experience of a friend of ours. Steve had come from a background similar to Jim's. He had used no sexual restraints and had been very promiscuous for a long time.

When he became a Christian he struggled diligently to maintain sexual purity. As a layman on our Christian education staff at church, he traveled with us and several others to a Christian education conference.

During the opening moments of one of the sessions, the leader had us stand and sing a song (one that should be banned from singles' meetings) which included verses saying:

. . . shake a little hand, shake the hand next to you . . .
. . . hug a little neck, hug the neck next to you . . .

When we got to the verse that says, ". . . scratch a little back, scratch the back next to you," Steve knew that he was becoming overstimulated. He turned to the female sitting next to him and in a very serious tone muttered, "If you touch my back, I'll kill you!"

Develop the following work sheet to establish your spiritual attitude about sexuality:

I recognize that I have been created with a strong sex drive. I commit this emotion to God and intend to avoid the negative pitfalls of this sex drive by developing positive responses to scriptural principles:

My Specific Negative Temptations and Pitfalls

Positive Scripture Portions Which Will Give Me Victory

Determine to remember that just any old Christian isn't good enough.

Many times the only qualification we place on the eligibility of someone of the opposite sex is, Is he or she a Christian?

That's just not enough. We need to plan our activities carefully, and select our dates just as carefully. We can be as easily unequally yoked with a believer as we can be with an unbeliever.

We must learn to be discerning in our selection of special friends. Consider the following criteria:

• Does this person love the Lord as much as I do?

• Is this person as committed to spiritual principles as I am?

• Is this person open to the will of God?

• Is this person more interested in developing his/her relationship with God than his/her relationship with me?

• Will this person communicate with me about sexuality?

• Will this person respect my convictions regarding my own sexual purity?

• Is this person willing to seek the advice and counsel of my spiritual parents?

Determine to develop a spiritual attitude regarding your sexuality.

There are four important components to a good attitude toward sexuality:

1. God created me with a strong sex drive.

"God created man in his own image, in the image of God he created him; male and female he created them" (Genesis 1:27).

Sex is not something that people *do*. Sex is something that people *are*—male and female.

We will never be successful in sexual purity if we try to get rid of our sexual feelings, or try to compartmentalize our sexuality to the attic of our lives.

2. God created me for marriage.

"At the beginning of creation God made them male and female. For this reason a man will leave his father and mother and be united to his wife, and the two will become one flesh. So they are no longer two, but one" (Mark 10:6–8).

God has designed us for the marriage relationship. The very emotions that give us the greatest difficulties as single individuals will be the ones we need to make our marriage relationship everything God intends it to be.

3. God expects me to control sexual passions until marriage.

"Do not let sin reign in your mortal body so that you obey its evil desires" (Romans 6:12).

"To the pure, all things are pure, but to those who are corrupted and do not believe, nothing is pure. In fact, both their minds and consciences are corrupted" (Titus 1:15).

"You have heard that it was said, 'Do not commit adultery.' But I tell you that anyone who looks at a woman lustfully has already committed adultery with her in his heart. If your right eye causes you to sin, gouge it out and throw it away. It is better for you to lose one part of your body than for your whole body to be thrown into hell. And if your right hand causes you to sin, cut it off and throw it away. It is better for you to lose one part of your body than for your whole body to go into hell" (Matthew 5:27–30).

4. Daily I will bring my concerns about sexuality to God.

"Humble yourselves, therefore, under God's mighty hand, that he may lift you up in due time. Cast all your anxiety on him because he cares for you. Be self-controlled and alert. Your enemy the devil prowls around like a roaring lion looking for someone to devour. Resist him, standing firm in the faith, because you know that your brothers throughout the world are undergoing the same kind of sufferings" (1 Peter 5:6–9).

There's one final thing I feel needs to be said with regard to sexual purity.

I have known many sincere single-again people who have struggled with this issue. They have allowed their failures to make them feel unworthy of God's love and grace to them. And so at the exact time when they needed God's help most—they moved away from Him rather than toward Him.

Do you really understand what happens when you come to the Lord in repentance? God forgives us completely—as if we had never sinned!

We must commit our sexual needs to the Lord. Then we must believe that Jesus is on our side. Jesus doesn't want us to repress our sexual needs—to ignore them—or become slaves to them. Jesus wants to redeem us and our sexuality. Jesus wants to make us whole.

Just as Jesus pointed out to the Pharisees that the sabbath was made for man, rather than man being made for the sabbath (see Mark 2:23–28), so sex was made for us—we were not made for sex. It is not a drive that we cannot control.

I understand that God created me for marriage. I recognize the desire I have for marriage and commit this to the Lord. Even above a marriage relationship, I desire a committed relationship with my Lord and will allow Him to direct me in this area.

Ways I Was Created for Marriage

I understand the restraints God has placed on His people in the area of sexual purity. I covenant with God to control my sexual passions.

Steps I Will Take to Maintain My Sexual Purity

I will pray daily for God's help in this area.

My Daily Prayer to God

7

The Therapy of Forgiveness

Chapter Focus

God's miracle gift to you is forgiveness. You can learn the principles of forgiveness that will help you live in freedom from guilt.

What God's Word Says

"If you, O Lord, kept a record of sins, O Lord, who could stand? But with you there is forgiveness; therefore you are feared. . . . O Israel, put your hope in the Lord, for with the Lord is unfailing love and with him is full redemption" (Psalm 130:3–4,7).

Vignette

When I met my husband, Jim, he was a man with a past filled with years of sin. For the prior fifteen years he had been a heroin addict on the streets of Chicago, involved in every kind of sin imaginable. He had been an alcoholic as well, and to support his addictive life-style he had become a criminal, spending much time in jails. He had married and divorced not once but four times.

On January 21, 1972, Jim knelt before the Lord and prayed a very simple prayer: "God, I don't know much about you, but if you make me happy like these Christians here [at Chicago Teen Challenge], I'll do anything you want me to do."

God administered His therapy of forgiveness, and when we said our vows on June 2, 1973, I married a brand new creature in Christ!

I thank God that I don't have to worry about getting up every morning and living in fear of finding used hypodermic needles in my sink. I don't check the garbage to find empty whiskey bottles. I have never once walked into my living room to find stolen goods, nor have I, even once, felt condemned by the sin of adultery for marrying a divorced man. Because I didn't. I didn't marry a heroin addict. I didn't marry an alcoholic. I didn't marry a criminal. I didn't marry a divorced man. I married a brand new baby saint. All God remembers about Jim Dycus is what he has done since January 21, 1972. He's a man with no past.

One of the greatest gifts God ever gave to humankind is His therapy of forgiveness. Without it we would live in a constant state of guilt that could never be removed.

A load of guilt bound Jim to a fifteen-year drug addiction. Hospitals and rehabilitation programs couldn't remove the guilt. Countless psychologists and psychiatrists couldn't point the way to a guilt-free conscience. It was a bondage that only God's therapy of forgiveness could eradicate from his life.

Jim describes the bondage in the following way:

> I've been bound; I know how it feels. Satan bound me to my past, led me down a path of total destruction until I lay in the pit of hell, broken and despised by everyone I knew. Then he threw that past in front of me, not once but millions of times. The daily parade of pain that I endured for years—all the faces of people I had hurt passing through my memory—bound me hopelessly to the evil, taunting control of Satan.
>
> The problem I had wasn't heroin; it was Satan and his chains of sin. The single most important thing that I could share with you is the news that Satan doesn't hold those keys that lock you in your bondage. Christ does! When He died on that lonely hill of Calvary, He got off that cross and walked into the very pit of hell to confront Satan and grab the keys from him. Then He used them to open my chains and your chains, and to let the captives go free.

"If the Son therefore shall make you free, Ye shall be free indeed!" (John 8:36, KJV).

God was able to completely eradicate all the bondages of my old life. Greater than that, He was able to take those bondages and turn them into stepping stones to my greatest victories.

That's what God's forgiveness does—it removes the chains of guilt that bind us to our sinful past. That is why it is so vitally important for us to understand this wonderful gift. As God gives the gift to us, we can pass it on to others who need it too.

I was raised in a Christian home. My parents protected me from all the evil influences of the world around me. I wasn't even allowed to have a deck of Old Maid cards. I'm not sure if they really thought playing cards would be an evil influence, or if they just feared playing Old Maid would make me one! But I never learned to play the game.

As my parents protected me from even the knowledge of evils present in my world, my mother encouraged me to read the Bible. "Read it every night before you go to sleep" she would tell me, "and it will protect you from Satan's influences."

So I read it almost nightly. Many nights as I read I felt as though I ought to pull the covers up over my head and read with a flashlight in case my mother discovered what I was reading.

Do you know that every sin that any human being ever has committed or ever will commit is discussed in God's Word? And often it's the saints of God that commit the sins.

The Bible is filled with lust, rape, murder, homosexuality, incest, betrayal, divorce, perversion, adultery, and embezzlement. I often wondered if my mother really knew what she was encouraging me to read. I wondered why Abraham, David, Isaac, Jacob, Paul, and other saints committed those sins. Yet God loved them and used them in powerful ways.

Why? God wants us to know that there isn't any sin that any human being can dream up that hasn't already been thought of and committed by people who have gone on to become mighty men and women of God because of His gift of forgiveness!

Look up each of the Scripture references given below. Write a brief statement explaining who sinned, what sin the individual committed, and how God responded.

Exodus 2:11–15

2 Samuel 11:1–27; 12:1–24

Acts 9:1–20

Before we consider the principles of forgiveness, we are going to look at the motivation for forgiveness. What was it that prompted God to be willing to freely offer this gift to sinners?

Throughout the Old Testament, men and women struggled to live within the standards of God's law only to fail time after time. The Law was holy, just, and impossible to keep. The judgment for breaking the Law was severe. And the ritualistic attempts that people made to find absolution from that judgment were woefully inadequate.

Thus a better plan was needed. God sent His own Son to earth to complete this plan. Through Jesus Christ's death on the cross the weight of sin was lifted from the backs of imperfect men and women.

Colossians 2:13–15 describes this better plan: "When you

were dead in your sins and in the uncircumcision of your sinful nature, God made you alive with Christ. He forgave us all our sins, having canceled the written code, with its regulations, that was against us and that stood opposed to us; he took it away, nailing it to the cross. And having disarmed the powers and authorities, he made a public spectacle of them, triumphing over them by the cross."

God's forgiveness—prompted by His mercy and grace—is God's better plan!

For me, James 2:13 sums it up: "Mercy triumphs over judgment!"

I heard a speaker define God's mercy and grace in this way: "God's grace is God giving us what we don't deserve. God's mercy is God not giving us what we do deserve."

A woman went to a photographer's studio to look at some portrait proofs that had been prepared for her. When she took the proofs from the photographer's hands and looked at them for the first time, she exclaimed: "My, these don't do me justice!" The photographer looked at the woman and then down at the proofs, contemplated for a moment, and replied: "Madam, it's not justice you need—it's mercy!" As do all of us!

It is God's great mercy and grace for us that prompted Him to introduce forgiveness. He desires to give the gift of forgiveness to each of us. The Bible tells us: "He devises ways so that a banished person may not remain estranged from him" (2 Samuel 14:14).

Think back to your experience with God's plan of forgiveness. What ways did God devise to reach you with this gift?

What evidence can you see of God's grace at work in this experience?

It is important to develop the concept of God's gift of forgiveness as it applies to the sin of divorce.

Divorce is still thought of as the unpardonable sin by many in the religious community. The stigma associated with divorced persons isn't found in the secular world. There divorce is just another sociological phenomenon—but in the religious community many struggle with this stigma.

A divorced person often is thought of as permanently scarred, tainted, and condemned. Often divorced people feel as though they belong in the bargain basement of the church with the rejects, the stained, and the irregulars.

Divorce is a sin. It was never intended to be a part of God's perfect plan for humankind. But so is gossip, arrogance, and pride. We must know there is a way to be restored to full fellowship with God no matter what our sin.

Dwight H. Small says, "The question of marital failure is like that of any other ethical failure in Christian experience; it is subject to God's grace expressed in realized forgiveness and renewal to life's highest possibilities again."

Check out the story of David's sin of murder, deception, and adultery. It was severe enough that God could have killed them both, or at least removed David from the throne and shut up Bathsheba's womb so she could have no more children.

But the postscript to the story of David and Bathsheba's sin is not found in 2 Samuel. It is found in the little-read first chapter of Matthew. Right in the middle of the genealogy of God's own Son, Jesus, we read this verse:

"David was the father of Solomon, whose mother had been Uriah's wife [Bathsheba]" (Matthew 1:6).

God underscored His gift of forgiveness to David and Bathsheba by including them in the ancestry of His own Son, Jesus. God's forgiveness and mercy triumphed over the judgment of the law concerning their sin. Grace will always rise above the law!

I want to introduce you to five principles of forgiveness that will help you put away your past and reach for the meaningful future God has in store for you.

Forgetting Forgiven Sin

God continues to forgive the sins of those who seek to know Him. "'You will seek me and find me when you seek me with all your heart'" (Jeremiah 29:13), says the Lord. And He continues, "'They will all know me, from the least of them to the greatest,' declares the Lord. 'For I will forgive their wickedness and will remember their sins no more'" (Jeremiah 31:34).

We were made for fellowship with God. Those days after Adam and Eve were created, when they walked and talked in the Garden of Eden with God, were simply heaven on earth—and they were too few and too short!

But one of the unalterable characteristics of God the Father is His absolute refusal to look upon sin. So when someone sinned, as long as that sin remained unconfessed, God could not allow that person to fellowship with Him.

God made this clear to Moses. "Then the Lord appeared at the Tent in a pillar of cloud, and the cloud stood over the entrance to the Tent. And the Lord said to Moses: 'You are going to rest with your fathers, and these people will soon prostitute themselves to the foreign gods of the land they are entering. They will forsake me and break the covenant I made with them. On that day I will become angry with them and forsake them; I will hide my face from them, and they will be destroyed'" (Deuteronomy 31:15–17).

God reminded the people of this characteristic again through the prophet Isaiah. "Surely the arm of the Lord is not too short to save, nor his ear too dull to hear. But your iniquities have separated you from your God; your sins have hidden his face from you, so that he will not hear. For your hands are stained with blood, your fingers with guilt. Your lips have spoken lies, and your tongue mutters wicked things" (Isaiah 59:1–3).

How God must have longed for fellowship with His creation. Thus the first step of His promise of forgiveness was to create a plan whereby that fellowship could be restored.

Our key verse tells us about that first step. It involves the dual components of forgiving and forgetting. Forgiveness is never complete without forgetfulness.

God could not forgive alone. He needed a way to eradicate the memory of the person's sin, so as He restored that person to fellowship with himself, He would not see the sin. This was completed through God's choice to forget as well as to forgive the sin.

Forgetting forgiven sin is a key element in the process. God forgives and forgets my sin just as I must forgive and forget my own sin and the sin of others.

With this first step in the process of forgiveness God has created a way to restore the fellowship which He desires to have with us. He can bring us back up to "sit with Him in heavenly places." The stain and scars of sin are no longer present. He can see me, but He cannot see my sins.

I remember the story of a nun who went to visit her bishop, claiming she had had a supernatural visitation from Jesus Christ. The bishop was skeptical and questioned her carefully. He decided to give her a further test. "Go back home," he told her, "and the next time Jesus Christ visits you, ask Him this question: What was the bishop's greatest sin before you forgave him?"

A few weeks later the nun returned to the bishop's office. "Bishop," she exclaimed, "I've had another visitation from Jesus Christ."

"Did you remember what I told you to ask Him?" asked the bishop.

"Yes, I did," she replied.

"Well, what was His answer?" the bishop asked rather warily.

"Jesus said, 'I don't remember the bishop's greatest sin,'" she replied immediately.

When God forgives . . . He forgets!

What are the sins you have committed which you are having difficulty forgetting? Do you find it hard to believe that God has really forgiven you?

99

Pray this prayer:

"Lord, I find it so hard to believe You have really forgiven me for all my failures and sins. But I believe Your Word, and it tells me that You will 'remember [my] sins no more' (Hebrews 8:12).

"Help me to really believe in Your total forgiveness and forgetfulness. Help me to forgive myself, and then to begin to forget the failures and sins I remember so easily. Let me begin today to take this first step in Your wonderful process of forgiveness."

Removing Forgiven Sin

"As far as the east is from the west, so far has he removed our transgressions from us" (Psalm 103:12).

This is a particularly interesting verse when compared to the key verse in the first step of forgiveness.

Why, when we already have heard that God forgives our sin and promises to remember it no more, is it necessary for Him to remove it as far as the east is from the west?

Many times after God has forgotten those sins we have confessed, we remember them. They weigh on our minds, making our hearts heavy and hindering us from going beyond failure into what God has for us.

From the little bit I remember about elementary geography, if I were to travel north I could eventually meet the south; and if I were to travel south, I could eventually meet the north. The two directions come together at the poles, back to back. But if I drive straight east, I will never arrive at a point where west begins. I will always be heading east. And vice versa for driving west.

God knew the struggle we would have with forgetting our own sins. He realized the memories of failure could hinder us from ever reaching our potential in Christ. So in the process of forgiveness He included this step of reaching down to us, picking up that load of sin, and taking it far away from us—not as far as

100

the north is from the south—but "as far as the east is from the west."

This is a powerful step for two reasons. First, it frees us from past failure. In a moment's time we are liberated, no longer encumbered by past sin.

This is the way my husband, Jim, describes that moment:

> I stayed there on my knees for a long time. Something was happening deep inside me, where I'd been dead for so many years. Feelings I hadn't felt since I was a little boy were rushing over me. Others that I had never felt and couldn't explain were bursting forth. I couldn't move, but I felt as if I was flying high, felt that nothing could pull me back down into my pain. I got up feeling like Mr. Clean. The pain was gone! I felt free, light, released like a prisoner from bondage.

It is a life-changing moment when we recognize that God has removed the weight of sin.

But there is another reason why this step is so important to us. Often during counseling people I have heard such statements as this:

"If I ever sin, it will be in this area, because I've always been weak there. I fell there before and I have to be so careful because that is my weak spot."

I don't believe in that kind of theology! God does not eradicate our sins only to leave us weak in that area, with a tendency to sin there again.

Think about the key verse for this step. "As far as the east is from the west, so far hath he removed our sins from us."

Catch the spiritual picture God wants you to see in that verse. Your sin is gone! As long as you head east (toward the risen Son), you will never reach that western setting sun of failure— and it won't reach you either.

Have you been guilty of believing you have a weak area—a place where you've failed before and probably will again?

What is that area?

Now get a black crayon and scribble over the words you just wrote. Or you might cut the words out, and over the hole, tape a piece of clean white paper with these words:

"Gone—as far as the east is from the west!"

Forgetting the Sins of Others

"Who is a God like unto thee, that pardoneth the iniquity, and passeth by the transgression of the remnant of his heritage. . . . He will turn again, he will have compassion upon us; he will subdue our iniquities; and thou wilt cast all their sins into the depths of the sea" (Micah 7:18–19, KJV).

An encyclopedia will tell you about portions of the Pacific Ocean being more than 30,000 feet deep. In Micah's day, that was so far down no one could ever see what was on the bottom.

But that was before today's technology. Now we can reach the bottom of the sea. That thought kind of changes the meaning of this verse in Micah. Just as someone remembering my sin changes how forgiven I feel.

If God forgets sin—we must forget sin also! Yet so many times we remember the sins of another. We make value judgments about that person's worth based on his or her past failures. We have no right to do that.

In the area of divorce such "memory work" by others becomes one of the biggest stumbling blocks to the divorced and forgiven. Individuals, as well as churches, are sometimes guilty of basing judgment of a person on the circumstances of past failure and divorce.

I remember when I first began dating Jim. I recognized from the beginning that Jim and I came from vastly different backgrounds. I had been raised in a Christian environment, had gone to Bible school right after high school, and was in full-time ministry when I met Jim. I was waiting for a twentieth-century version of Daniel or Martin Luther for my mate. What a dilemma when God sent Jim!

The more time we spent together the more I heard about

Jim's past. Even though I knew from the start that God was doing something special in our relationship, the knowledge of his past began to affect me. How could I think about stepping to the altar of matrimony with a man that had been to that altar four times already? How could I believe that after fifteen years of drug and alcohol addiction this nine-month old baby Christian would never slip back into old habits? How could he establish a lasting relationship with a woman when he had known hundreds of women in his past, and never cultivated a real relationship with any of them? What would this man ever make of himself?

One night, alone in a motel room in Los Angeles, I seemed to hear God whisper in my ear, "Barbara, you have two choices: You can go on indulging in your carnal curiosity about Jim's past, asking hundreds of questions and developing recurring doubts about what I can do with his future. Or you can be like Me, spiritually senile, forgetting his past and never letting it become an obstacle to the future I am giving you with Jim."

I chose to become "spiritually senile." From that time on I never asked Jim questions about his past and never let my knowledge of his past affect the present and future that we have together.

Let me share Jim's response to my decision to become spiritually senile.

> And because she did, willingly believing in my less-than-year-old faith in God, I was able to begin learning to trust myself. Her gift of trust put legs on my faith, and through the power of the Holy Spirit and Barb's trust I no longer was afraid to walk away from my past. I was free to live fully in the bright and hopeful new future that God had given to me.

I believe I see the prophet Micah making the same choice. Look at Micah 7:19 again, and notice his switch from third person singular "he" to second person singular "thou":

"He will turn again, he will have compassion upon us; he will subdue our iniquities; and thou wilt cast all their sins into the depths of the sea " (KJV).

Why the switch? Was Micah just a poor grammar student, or is there a spiritual lesson God wants us to glean from this verse? I think there is. Imagine with me this background:

Micah was a preacher. This verse finds him in his church on Sunday morning, delivering his sermon to his parishioners. Micah was a very good pastor, and during the preceding week he had spent much time counseling his people. He knew that Thaddeus was being unfaithful to his wife. He knew that Deborah was sneaking around with the baker down the street. He recognized that Levi was becoming more and more addicted to the temple wine. He knew just about every failure and weakness of the members of his congregation.

He agonized for his people. If only he could point them to God whom he knew would forgive their transgressions and remove them from their bondage forever. As he preached, his eyes were on the congregation but his thoughts were on his great God up in heaven. In great earnestness he began:

"He will turn again, he will have compassion upon us; he will subdue our iniquities; and. . ."

Right there, mid-sentence, God stopped Micah and whispered into his ear: "Micah, look at me, I'm here; I am in the presence of my people. Remember the great salvation I brought to *you* as well as to the congregation."

Then, gloriously aware of the miracle of salvation he had experienced, becoming conscious of the God of his salvation, Micah drops off talking about God and addresses Him directly: ". . . and thou wilt cast all their sins into the depths of the sea."

It makes us a whole lot more tolerant of another's failure if, like Micah (and his contemporary Isaiah—see Isaiah 6:5), we are much more mindful of our failure in the eyes of a holy God!

Whose sins do you have trouble forgetting?

Each time you are tempted to recall another's sin, remember that you have no right to another's past. You don't even have a right to your own! Focus on God, and take your eyes off your sins or your brother's (or your former spouse's).

104

List the things that God has done for you since you asked His forgiveness:

Bringing Life Out of Death

"Therefore, if any man be in Christ, he is a new creature, old things are passed away; behold all things are become new" (2 Corinthians 5:17, KJV).

When I hear the words "passed away," I assume a funeral has taken place. And so it has! God is a thorough God. He isn't content with forgiving our sin and then forgetting it. He isn't content with taking it as far away from us as the east is from the west. He isn't even content with burying it in the deepest sea—someone might come along and dredge it up.

God doesn't consider the job complete until He buries that old life, full of sin and failure, and births a new baby Christian.

Dr. Harold Ivan Smith is so succinct on this point: "We ought to be holding a memorial service, then sending out birth announcements."

We aren't the same people we used to be. We died and were buried in the process of forgiveness. God has created us brand new people, ready to grow up and become the godly people He intends for us to be.

That's why I need never have feared Jim's past. The man I know is the new Jim Dycus. The old one I have never met. In the many years I have known Jim, I have never seen anything in him that resembles that other man. When we met, I could not believe he had ever been the man he told me about, and I still cannot. God has completely removed every shred of evidence that he ever existed. I believe there is no man better able than Jim Dycus to shout forth the message that God can set the captives free. Jim Dycus has been set free. God has declared him not guilty.

105

Take a plain piece of paper. On it write a description of the person you used to be before forgiveness. Now fold the paper and burn it. Place the ashes in a box, take it outside and bury it.

Now pray this prayer:

"God, thank You for Your great gift of forgiveness. Thank You for taking that old, sinful self I used to be and giving me the chance to be a brand new person. I've buried that old person and I'm a brand new baby. Nurture me and teach me to become the person You've created me to be."

Moving Ahead with Life

"Brothers, I do not consider myself yet to have taken hold of it. But one thing I do: Forgetting what is behind and straining toward what is ahead, I press on toward the goal to win the prize for which God has called me heavenward" (Philippians 3:13–14).

I love this portion of God's Word. I've known many people who have walked through the process of forgiveness all the way up to this point and still feel like failures because they can't forget their past.

The apostle Paul was one of those people. He struggled with the memory of the man he used to be. He's the one who said in Romans 7:24: "What a wretched man I am! Who will rescue me from this body of death?"

We will never be able to open the door to the new life Christ has for us if we can't close the door on our forgiven and forgotten past. But how do we do it? How can we forget the miserable, contemptible person we used to be? What do we do when even our sleep is interrupted with dreams and memories of our past?

Once again, the secret is in what Paul wrote in Philippians 3. How many things did Paul say he was going to do? "This one thing I do." But then if you look carefully at the remainder of his sentence you see him doing two things: "Forgetting . . . and reaching forth."

106

Let me share the Dycus paraphrase of this verse:

"I know I haven't arrived yet. I can't even forget the despicable bum I used to be. But I want to forget, so I'm just going to do this one thing (after I forget my past, that is). I'm going to stretch as hard as I can toward being the man God believes I can be."

Paul may have been struggling with his past, but there is no sin in such a struggle. He knew that the best way to struggle through to victory was to put all his energies and abilities into doing what God wanted him to do right then.

If we are trying to become the person God wants us to be, it will keep us so busy we won't have time to worry about the person we used to be.

The only requirement God makes is that we let loose completely of our past and allow Him to move us ahead to the new life He has for us.

Several biblical characters realized the importance of letting go of the past and moving ahead in their lives.

• The woman at the well of Samaria came to Jesus with an empty water pot, looking for physical water. When He spoke to her of spiritual water, her life was transformed. A key verse in her story is John 4:28–29: "Then leaving her water jar, the woman went back to the town and said to the people, 'Come, see a man who told me everything I ever did. Could this be the Christ?'"

• Mary Magdalene stood sorrowing at the empty tomb on Easter Sunday. She mourned the loss of her Lord. As she stared at the empty tomb, someone asked her why she was crying. Thinking it was the gardener, she asked where he had taken the body of her Lord. Then the miracle occurred: "She turned toward him and cried out, . . . 'Teacher!'" (John 20:16). As she turned from the pain of her loss she recognized her Lord. But it took turning away from the pain in order to see Jesus for who He is.

• Two fishermen stood by the seaside fishing one day. A man approached them and offered a better deal. "You've been fishing for live fish and they've been dying," Jesus said to them. "Come follow me and I'll teach you to fish for dead men and I'll make them live again. At once they left their nets and followed him" (Matthew 4:20, Dycus paraphrase).

•Not every biblical character was able to move forward into this new life and leave the past behind. A young man came to Jesus one day, empty and confused by a life that seemed to have no meaning. "Teacher, what good thing must I do to get eternal life?" he asked Jesus.

The Bible tells us what happened next: "Jesus answered, 'If you want to be perfect, go, sell your possessions and give to the poor, and you will have treasure in heaven. Then come, follow me.' When the young man heard this, he went away sad, because he had great wealth" (Matthew 19:21–22).

Maybe we don't have great wealth. Maybe we have "great" memories of past failure which we aren't able to release to God. In order to become the person God wants us to be, we have to put all our energies and efforts into moving forward, not looking backward.

We're all familiar with the story of Jekyll and Hyde. Dr. Jekyll stood at his laboratory table one evening, holding a vial of chemical which he had created. He believed it had a potential for good. Since both his assistant and his dog had made a mad dash for the door when they saw that vial, no one was there to test it. So he decided to test it on himself.

Dr. Jekyll turned into the raging Mr. Hyde, and went out into the street creating havoc. When the effects of the drug began to wear off, he stumbled back into his laboratory and once again grasped that vial of chemical in his hand. At that moment he was faced with the most important decision he would ever make. He could dash that vial against the wall and destroy its potential for evil; or he could experiment further to see if he could find a good use for that evil chemical.

Dr. Jekyll chose foolishly—he kept the vial. Each time he experimented he became a more violent Mr. Hyde. Finally he lost the ability to turn back into the intelligent and humane Dr. Jekyll.

We have the same choice to make about our past. There is no good thing that will ever come of our past. It will only continue to hinder us and destroy our potential for fulfilling God's design for us. We must choose to turn our backs on the past and stretch forth to the bright, new future that God has for us through His therapy of forgiveness.

We need to offer this opportunity to others who need to hear about God's plan for forgiveness—even to those who were instrumental in inflicting great pain on us! They can't hurt us anymore. Our past is gone, and until their past is gone they can't become the people God wants them to be.

Maybe you can be the one to give them that hope!

8

Positive Choices About Negative Things

Chapter Focus

Through the Word of God we can learn the skills necessary to break down walls of negative emotion and gather the building blocks of positive adjustment. These positive emotional responses will build a stronghold of recovery.

What God's Word Says

"Forget the former things; do not dwell on the past. See, I am doing a new thing! Now it springs up; do you not perceive it? I am making a way in the desert and streams in the wasteland" (Isaiah 43:18–19).

"Brothers [and sisters], whatever is true, whatever is noble, whatever is right, whatever is pure, whatever is lovely, whatever is admirable—if anything is excellent or praiseworthy—think about such things" (Philippians 4:8).

Vignette

In our divorce recovery workshops for children we present a lesson on turning despair to hope with the help of Prince Despair and Princess Hope.

Prince Despair comes into view dressed in black, raining down despair and hopelessness on all his shadow passes. In despair, he sings:

Little children, despair, you're a child of divorce
Despair, you're a child of divorce,
Despair, you're a child of divorce.
Hang your head down low, despair,
You're a child of divorce.

Then as the doom and gloom settles over everyone, suddenly in the back of the room a small, cheerful voice is heard singing:

Little children, rejoice, you're a child of the King,
Rejoice, you're a child of the King.
Rejoice, you're a child of the King.
Lift your head up high, rejoice, you're a child of the King.

As Princess Hope makes her way through the crowd, getting closer and closer to Prince Despair, he begins to cower. Each time she sings the word, "Rejoice," he sinks further to the ground. The kids join her and soon the whole room of kids is screaming: "Rejoice . . . rejoice . . . rejoice!"

What a lesson for us adults! A crisis doesn't need to burden our lives and cause us to hang our heads in sorrow and hurt. Through God's grace we can learn to lift our heads high and build a positive life beyond our negative experiences.

We can gather our spiritual building blocks and begin to construct a stronghold of wholeness. We will do this by identifying the negative emotional walls that must be demolished, and then putting in their place positive building blocks to recovery.

Emotional Wall: Grief

Building Block: Hope

If ever there was an example of a grief-stricken individual it is King David as recorded in Psalm 31! "My life is consumed by anguish and my years by groaning; my strength fails because of my affliction, and my bones grow weak" (v. 10).

Anyone who has experienced loss has experienced grief. That is normal. But when grief paralyzes our emotions and robs us of our recovery, then grief is blocking our recovery and is ready for demolition.

111

In Psalm 31 David gives us the pattern for using the biblical block of hope to crush grief: "Praise be to the Lord, for he showed his wonderful love to me when I was in a besieged city. In my alarm I said, 'I am cut off from your sight!' Yet you heard my cry for mercy when I called to you for help" (vv. 21–22).

The block of hope, acting much like "the stone the builders rejected" (Luke 20:17–18), will break the paralysis of grief every time. God longs to help rebuild our lives with hope. David said it best in verse 24: "Be strong and take heart, all you who hope in the Lord!"

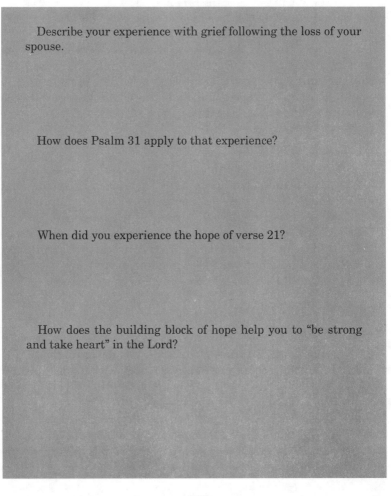

Describe your experience with grief following the loss of your spouse.

How does Psalm 31 apply to that experience?

When did you experience the hope of verse 21?

How does the building block of hope help you to "be strong and take heart" in the Lord?

Emotional Wall: Loss

Building Block: Stability

Second Kings 4:1–7 records the story of a family that became immobilized by the death of the husband and father. As adversity piled upon adversity, it seemed as though they would die too. The paralysis of negative emotion always makes us think that! It puts us in a losing frame of mind: we anticipate and expect more adversity and its consequences.

I saw a picture of a huge Douglas fir tree that had been uprooted by a storm. The tree lay on the ground, its enormous root system exposed to the elements. A small portion of the root, however, remained firmly in the ground and had proved adequate support for continued growth of the huge tree. Apparently years had passed since the original storm, for the picture recorded an amazing thing: That tree trunk, leveled as it was, had indeed begun growing again. The trunk had straightened back up into the sun, once again standing tall, its branches full and firmly established.

Through the counsel of Elisha, that single-parent family in 2 Kings 4 learned to do the same thing. Elisha in effect advised them to take their focus off their adversity and put it on adjustment to their crisis. As that single mother and her sons did so, stability was restored to that home. New growth began to occur because of that stability coming from their adjustment.

They found strength in their ability to respond positively to their negative crisis. It's when we find our inner sources of strength that we can grow. A life uprooted by crisis can still reach its potential when turned over to Christ.

Think about the beautiful words of this old song.

> He giveth more grace when the burdens grow greater;
> He sendeth more strength when the labors increase.
> To added affliction, He addeth His mercy,
> To multiplied trials, His multiplied peace.
>
> When we have exhausted our store of endurance,
> When our strength has failed ere the day is half done,
> When we reach the end of our hoarded resources,
> Our Father's full giving is only begun.

For His love has no limits, His grace has no measure;
His power has no boundary known unto men.
For out of His infinite riches in Jesus, He giveth, and giveth,
and giveth again.

That's what this widow and her children discovered about God. When their loss had dissipated and stability was restored in their home, they recognized that God was greater than their negative circumstances.

Look again at Elisha's instruction in verse 7. "Go, sell the oil and pay your debts. You and your sons can live on what is left." God's resources are always sufficient for our daily lives!

Describe your attempts to restore stability after your loss.

When did you recognize the resources of God helping you create a whole, growing, stable life-style for you and your family?

Emotional Wall: Guilt

Building Block: Assurance

In 1 Corinthians 6:9–11, Paul points out that "the wicked will not inherit the kingdom of God," and gives examples of what he means by "wicked": the sexually immoral, adulterers, male prostitutes, homosexual offenders, drunkards. Then he says, "That is what some of you were" (v. 11).

No one among the Corinthian believers had grown up in the church. They had been some of Paul's earliest converts and, at one time, had lived sinful, evil lives. But he reminds them that they "were washed, . . . sanctified, . . . justified in the name of the Lord Jesus Christ" (v. 11). In so doing, he says in effect: "God's mercy has absolved your guilt!"

So many people struggle with guilt in their lives. When victorious Christians exclaim, "God has completely removed all my guilt!" hosts of other struggling Christians quietly respond, "Yeah, easy for you to say. You don't know how guilty I am!"

But you don't know how forgiven you are!

Paul knew how forgiven Christians are. He knew how forgiven he was! He remembered God's application of mercy to his life, and he applied knowledge of that mercy to those he wrote to. Read, for example, Colossians 1:13–14: "[God] has rescued us from the dominion of darkness and brought us into the kingdom of the Son he loves, in whom we have redemption, the forgiveness of sins."

As we read these verses in Colossians, we can catch a glimpse of the thoroughness of God's mercy. It doesn't just bring us inside the door of salvation and then leave us there as second-class citizens of the kingdom. It gives us the privilege of growing in our salvation.

It offers us the privilege of
• Being filled "with the knowledge of his will"
• "Spiritual wisdom and understanding"
• Pleasing God "in every way"
• "Bearing fruit in every good work"
• "Growing in the knowledge of God"
• "Being strengthened with all power"
• Having "great endurance and patience"
• "Joyfully giving thanks to the Father"
• Being "qualified . . . to share in the inheritance of the saints in the kingdom of the light"

Forget the past, forget the guilt, forget the sense of worthlessness—we are new creations and coheirs with Christ.

Do you struggle with guilt for past sins? God's mercy will help you eradicate that guilt from your life and move ahead to becoming the person God wants you to be.

Apply the following benefits to your life. Be very specific. How would these benefits change your life? Where do you need them most? How will you be different with them?

Knowledge of His Will

Spiritual Wisdom

Spiritual Understanding

Pleasing God in Every Way

Bearing Fruit in Every Good Work

Growing in the Knowledge of God

Great Endurance

Great Patience

Joyfully Giving Thanks to God

Qualified to Share the Inheritance of the Saints

Rescued from the Dominion of Darkness

Forgiveness of Sins

Emotional Wall: Rejection

Building Block: Acceptance

People who have been rejected need to be accepted! It is a simple fact, but difficult to achieve in broken lives.

Onesimus in the Book of Philemon can be an important guide in learning both how to accept others, and how to receive acceptance. There are several principles from this short book which are important to understand. First, rejection renders us useless and acceptance restores our sense of self-worth, giving us a platform from which to make a contribution once again. Through the ministry of Paul, restoration between Onesimus and Philemon was accomplished. "Formerly he [Onesimus] was useless to you, but now he has become useful both to you and to me" (v. 11).

Second, rejection makes us subject to pain, and people in pain make other people hurt! But as my wall of hurt is broken by the building block of acceptance, I can learn to accept others. And I will feel accepted by others. Acceptance frees us from the servitude of pain. Even my self-worth will increase, from feeling like everyone's slave to believing myself to be a beloved brother (or sister) of those I most want to accept me. Onesimus was "no longer . . . a slave, but . . . a dear brother" (v. 16).

Third, acceptance is more than something I just choose to give to others; it is a debt I owe to God. Paul told Onesimus' owner, Philemon, that he, Paul, would make good on whatever the runaway slave had taken: "I will pay it back—not to mention that you owe me your very self" (v. 19). God loves you so much that He requires that I love you too! And you must love me! Even more difficult to grasp is this: God loves the one that hurt you so much that He requires you to offer acceptance to that person.

Finally, rejection keeps me in crisis. Acceptance leads the way out, to total wholeness. Paul wrote, "Confident of your obedience, I write to you, knowing that you will do even more than I ask" (v. 21). The more acceptance I feel, the more I want to please God. Paul's acceptance of Onesimus had freed him to become a useful man of God. Listen to Paul's words regarding this former slave:

"I appeal to you for *my son,* Onesimus" (v. 10, emphasis added).

"He has become useful both to you and to me" (v. 11).

He "is my very heart" (v. 12).

"I would have liked to keep him with me so that he could take your place in helping me" (v. 13).

"He is very dear to me" (v. 16).

Have you been rejected? How does it make you feel?

Have you felt genuine acceptance? How does acceptance make you feel?

To whom do you need to give the gift of total acceptance?

Emotional Wall: Anger

Building Block: Peace

Anger is unquestionably a disruptive force in a person's life. It takes hold in one little area and then permeates every other aspect of that life. It becomes a habitual response, a response that occurs at the slightest provocation.

This resident anger often results from thwarted goals. For the person who has experienced the disruption of divorce, with all its accompanying changes, thwarted goals become part of life. In the midst of a crisis, negative response is quite normal. However, anger may keep us tied to our negative circumstances, unable to rise above them to move ahead with our lives.

Paul recognized this characteristic of anger and addressed it in his letter to the Philippian church. Philippians 4:4–9 is loaded with principles to break the bondage of anger and replace it with a peace that transcends human understanding.

My children and I often drive Jim to the airport and then pick him up when he returns. Airport schedules sometimes mean unexpected delays. As we waited one time recently, my daughter, Jackie, noticed a bird's nest built directly above the arrival and baggage area. This is a heavily congested area of the airport: People double-park, buses plunge in and out of traffic lanes, taxi drivers use their horns instead of their brakes.

Yet right here in the midst of all the confusion sat a lone mother bird caring for her three little nestlings. She seemed totally unaffected by the noise around her. This was the spot she had chosen to make her home and nurture her young. Not once did she scold at a blaring horn. Never once did she fly out in anger at the bus blowing all its exhaust in her babies' faces. She just sat there, chirping merrily; from time to time flying off to bring back a tasty worm for her young. What a picture of peace in the midst of confusion!

Paul gives some insights into how to develop peace in our lives. Read verses 8–9: "Whatever is true, whatever is noble, whatever is right, whatever is pure, whatever is lovely, whatever is admirable—if anything is excellent or praiseworthy—think about such things. Whatever you have learned or received or heard from me, or seen in me—put it into practice. And the God of peace will be with you."

What circumstances in your life make you angry?

Is anger something you easily put aside, or does it have a hold you can't seem to break?

Think about those circumstances that evoke anger in you. Apply the following biblical principles to them:
What is true of these circumstances?

Is there a noble aspect to any of them, which you can identify and cling to?

What are the "spiritual rights" of your circumstances? How will dwelling on these rights help to dissipate the wrong emotions that accompany these circumstances?

Identify the pure, lovely, admirable, excellent, and praiseworthy qualities of your circumstances.

Can you find the God of peace in your circumstances? How has He ministered His peace to you?

Emotional Wall: Inferiority

Building Block: Worth

The breakup of a family unit causes each family member to struggle with feelings of inferiority. Before long we feel like bargain basement goods, and even believe we deserve all the bad things happening to us.

Many single-again individuals find it hard to rise above their feelings of inferiority, impairing their relationship-building skills. God wants us to realize our worth in Him. Worth is established not because of who we are, but because of who He is! Ephesians 2:4–10 helps us see how God feels about us and gives us a sense of worth that our experiences have robbed us of.

Read what God has done for us because of His great love: "Because of his great love for us, God, who is rich in mercy, made us alive with Christ . . . raised us up with Christ and seated us with him. . . . For we are God's workmanship, created in Christ Jesus to do good works, which God prepared in advance for us to do" (Ephesians 2:4–7,10). Consider the words of verse 10: "Created in Christ Jesus to do good works, which God prepared in advance for us to do." In advance of what? Could it not mean that God has good works for you to do after this crisis in your life even as He did before your crisis?

What inferior feelings do you struggle to expel from your thought life?

How has God:

Raised you up?

Seated you with Him?

Expressed His kindness to you?

Consider all you know about God's attributes. What kind of workmanship do you think He produces?

What do you think the "good works" in Ephesians 2:10 might mean in your life?

Emotional Wall: Inflexibility

Building Block: Adaptability

In Romans 5:1–6 we find the principle for adapting to the changes of our lives. God shares some insight into the reasons for change. It is a whole lot easier to make changes when we understand the reasons for them. "Since we have been *justified* through faith, we have *peace* with God . . . we have *gained access* . . . into . . . grace . . . we *rejoice in the hope of the glory of God*" (Romans 5:1–2, emphasis added).

Not only does He share the reasons for change, but He also shares the results of the change. As we read of these results we cannot help but recognize the tremendous spiritual growth that will take place as these changes are made. "Suffering produces *perseverance;* perseverance, *character;* and character, *hope.* And hope does not disappoint us, because God *has poured out his love into our hearts* by the Holy Spirit, whom he has given us" (vv. 3–5, emphasis added).

And then, just to let us know He understands our inflexibility, the portion closes with these words: "You see, at just the right time, when we were still powerless, Christ died for the ungodly" (v. 6).

How has your crisis made you inflexible in the face of change?

Indicate how these biblical qualities have begun to be expressed in your life:

Perseverance:

Character:

Hope:

When did you feel most powerless?

Other emotional walls need to be demolished so positive adjustment may occur, but thinking about these first seven walls will teach us how to move beyond them.

In Ecclesiastes 3 many wonderful principles for overcoming negative emotions and building positive responses are given. Verse 7 is particularly important: ". . . a time to tear, and a time to mend." One commentary renders that verse this way, "A time to rend the garments, as upon occasion of some great grief, and a time to sew them again, in token that the grief is over."

Basic to that rendering is the thought of forward motion, a positive thrust ahead—in other words, an action that anticipates the future. Every crisis has a beginning and an end! With God's help we can put the pieces of our lives together in a new form.

Read the words of Jeremiah 32:40–41 (*Living Bible*): "I will make an everlasting covenant with them, promising never again to desert them, but only to do them good. I will put a desire into their hearts to worship me, and they shall never leave me. I will rejoice to do them good and will replant them in this land, with great joy."

Living positively in the midst of negative circumstances is possible!

What negative emotions or circumstances are you struggling with?

What positive steps can you take to be victorious over them?

Remember!
To you God has given:

Healing for all your hurts.
Insights to build a better life.
Love to give away.
New dreams to dare you to reach beyond where you have been.
Obstacles to overcome.
Scars to turn into stars.

To you God has given:

Possibilities unlimited.
For you the sky is the limit.
What matters is not where you have been—but where you are
    going!
Believe it—never stop believing,
The best is yet to come!

9

A Child's View of Divorce

Chapter Focus

To help your child you must see divorce through the eyes of a child. Only then can you understand your child's emotions and concerns.

What God's Word Says

"Then little children were brought to Jesus for him to place his hands on them and pray for them. But the disciples rebuked those who brought them. Jesus said, 'Let the little children come to me and do not hinder them, for the kingdom of heaven belongs to such as these.' When he had placed his hands on them, he went on from there" (Matthew 19:13–15).

"People were bringing little children to Jesus to have him touch them, but the disciples rebuked them. When Jesus saw this, he was indignant. He said to them, 'Let the little children come to me, and do not hinder them, for the kingdom of God belongs to such as these. I tell you the truth, anyone who will not receive the kingdom of God like a little child will never enter it.' And he took the children in his arms, put his hands on them and blessed them" (Mark 10:13–16).

Vignette

A little girl was busily entertaining her parents' adult visitor by lining up all her dolls and explaining the merits of each.

"This one walks when you take her by the hand. And you can make this one's hair grow long just by combing it with this special comb. This one talks to you and answers your questions when you push this button on her back."

"Tell me, sweetheart," the man asked when she was through, "which of these is your very favorite doll?"

Immediately she drew back and looked him in the eyes. Folding her arms in front of her she exclaimed, "I can't show you my very favorite doll?"

Finally after several moments of persuasion, she ran off to her bedroom to get her favorite doll. As she returned to the room the man looked at the doll in her arms and was thoroughly surprised. The favorite doll was a mess! One arm dangled by a few threads. The left foot had been chewed off by the family dog. The features on the plastic face had been washed and kissed off. The dress was dirty and torn in several places.

"But, sweetheart, when you have all these beautiful dolls why would that one be your favorite doll?"

She gently hugged the doll to her face. "This is my very favorite doll because if I didn't love it, no one would!"

That's the way I feel about children who have lost a parent by divorce. So many times these little ones are crying out for someone to love them and help them understand the misery in their lives. And yet instead of hearing their cries for help, we label them "belligerent" or "problem children," even "undisciplined little brats"!

Notice the word "Then" leading off the verse in Matthew. It connects the action taking place following that word with the action just before it, in this instance, Jesus speaking about divorce and His encouraging the children to come to Him.

I believe Jesus wanted to give His disciples (including us) an object lesson, that divorce is not just about adults—it's also about children, children who can easily become the victims of divorce—let's not forget the children! In fact, Jesus declared for all to hear that the kingdom of heaven belonged to them. No one was to hinder them from coming to Him to claim their rightful inheritance.

Yet today, hundreds of years after Jesus' admonition concerning little children, multiplied thousands of children throughout our nation are being ignored or pushed aside at the time of their greatest hurt.

If we don't love them, who will!

But to love them we have to understand them better.

I asked a friend of ours who does all our illustrations to prepare an overhead transparency for me to use in the presentation of my workshop on "A Child's View of Divorce." I didn't know exactly what I wanted, so I said, "Andy, just draw something that shows how a child must feel about divorce."

He sent back the artwork for me in a few days. When I saw what he had done, I was overwhelmed. He had depicted perfectly how a child feels. He had drawn a huge monster looming menacingly and angrily over a little boy. The monster had his arms raised over the boy's figure, threatening to destroy his very life. However, if you looked closely at the picture of the little boy you could discern that the monster was actually the little boy's own shadow as he stood in front of a lamp.

That is truly a child's view of divorce. Divorce is an ugly monster that looms over the child and seems to threaten that child's very life. But guess who controls the monster? The child does—and that is the very essence of what we need to teach children of divorce, that with God's help they can control the monster of divorce!

Although ultimately this chapter is for the children, it must be given to them through the loving nurturing of their parents. However, many parents struggle with guilt and sorrow because they have forced their children to become children of divorce. As a result, this can be a very tough chapter for a parent to work through. So as we begin, I want you to consider Psalm 139:16: "All the days ordained for me were written in your book before one of them came to be."

God knew every moment and every circumstance of your life before you were conceived. He knew every moment and every circumstance of your child's life before that precious little life was conceived. He decided that you were the best person to raise the child He gave you—even though He knew in advance every situation you would face.

So take courage as a single! God hasn't forsaken you. He

hasn't forsaken your children. He is going to give you the wisdom and knowledge that you need to bring your child into the full potential of what God has planned for your child's life. You will have to work through some negative factors in your child's life because of divorce, but God will bring you and your family to the other side of divorce.

Just be willing to face the negatives so you can move to the positive.

Jesus faced the negative situation of being tired and pressed by the crowd. He made the choice to go to the other side of the lake. The storm in the middle of the lake did not deter Him one bit from arriving at the other side of that lake. It won't deter you either.

How do you feel about your child having to face the divorce of his or her parents?

What effect has the knowledge that your child had no choice in the decision to divorce, and yet bears the consequences of that decision, had on you?

How has this been a negative experience for your child?

We will begin our look at a child's viewpoint of loss by considering some of the age-level symptoms. While children of any age may experience some of these symptoms, they are generally the major symptoms of the age mentioned.

As we look at some of these negatives, please remember this: These are normal distresses facing a child who has lost a parent. With proper intervention and nurturing, these children can move quickly to the positive side of adjustment to divorce.

Symptoms of Divorce Stress

The Preschooler

It is important to realize that to a child under the age of six, Mom and Dad are the center of the universe. The little one has not yet moved outside the home for large portions of his day (unless he has been in a day-care setting), and Mom and Dad are the two major adult influences on his life. They are his world. When one of those adults has left the child's life, half his world has been taken away. Add to this the fact that the child does not yet have the reasoning power to understand the emotional turmoil he feels. He cannot say: "I feel sad because Daddy is gone," or "I'm acting bad right now because I'm angry; I haven't seen Mommy in so long." The child cannot verbalize his hurts as can older children.

The preschool child has specific needs during this time. He or she has the need for excessive physical affection. This little child will beg to be held and cuddled. He will cling to his remaining parent and latch on to any adult willing to give that needed affection.

I remember Jack, a little boy who attended our workshops several years back. He was a stranger to our church and had just lost his mom through divorce three weeks before his first night at the workshops.

His dad brought him to the door of the class for three- and four-year-olds. We use those wonderful half doors which allow a child to peer over but not escape out the door. We have coached our single parents to drop their kids off quickly and leave as soon as possible. We are prepared to handle the parting tears, but we don't want to prolong the scene.

His dad put Jack down on the floor, spoke briefly with the teacher, and began to walk down the hall from the room. This little fellow watched his dad leaving and wailed loudly for him as long as he could see him in the hallway. Then when his dad turned a corner out of his sight, the little boy turned around and observed the classroom.

The teacher already had begun the class and was sitting on the floor with the rest of the little ones in a circle around her. Little Jack looked over the situation: Catching sight of the teacher there on the floor, he made a mad dash for her. Jumping into her lap, wrapping his arms and legs around her, he buried his face in her neck and clung to her this way during the rest of the lesson. He had never seen this teacher before, had never been in that room before, yet he somehow understood that she could meet his need for physical affection.

As parents we must remember this is a real need in our young children. We are so quick to say, "Oh, hurry and grow up," or "I don't have time to hold you right now—go play in your room."

Many parents going through the crisis of loss struggle to meet this need in their little ones. This need for excessive affection comes at a time when the parent is emotionally drained and finds it difficult to nurture.

Another need common to preschoolers is that of guidance in social behaviors. Children this age are just discovering that the world doesn't revolve around them. There are other children to share toys with, there are big sisters and big brothers to deal with, and there are strangers of all ages who don't seem to realize preschoolers exist. It is not uncommon for the young child to have difficulty getting along with peers. The child hurts emotionally and does not understand what is causing the pain, perhaps thinking simply, *If all these other kids would just go away and leave me alone, I would feel better!*

It is important to monitor peer-group experiences for this child. Provide times of peer interaction with lots of supervision. Give guidance about the way to get along with friends. Be understanding when such children want to be alone or want all the toys. Use those moments to provide some physical nurturing, then release them back to peer play with their emotional tank "all filled up."

Preschoolers also have a great need to have their self-esteem built up. Mommy and Daddy were the whole world. Now Daddy is gone. "It must be because I'm not lovable enough. Maybe I'm so bad Mommy will go away too. She sure is gone more than she used to be, and she doesn't seem to want me around much either."

We must try to think like these little ones—put ourselves in their place—to gain some comprehension of their low self-esteem.

We also need to be aware that these three symptoms are normal for the preschooler. They will pass as the child's security is restored.

The Elementary-Age Child

The elementary-age child who always has been very well behaved in school may now begin to exhibit behavior problems. The teacher may send home a note requesting a conference, "because I just don't understand why your child is acting this way in my class." Then when the day of the meeting arrives, the teacher says, "Your child must have simply been having some bad days. Now she seems back to normal in her behavior."

Your child is experiencing varied and intense emotional stress. Some days this emotional stress is easier to understand and handle than on other days. "Bad days" are as much a reality to the child as to the parent. This emotional struggle may cause a temporary drop in grades. It is extremely helpful to develop good communication with the child's teacher and to keep the teacher informed of the child's progress toward recovery. Many teachers can be extremely helpful and supportive during this stressful time.

The elementary child is likely to become irritable and moody, especially at home. This may carry over into peer relationships, causing spats between the child and his friends. Let parents of your child's closest friends know of these changes. Encourage your child to express feelings verbally to you.

The elementary child will experience difficulty focusing and staying on tasks both in school and at home. He may appear aimless and easily discouraged.

These sets of symptoms can be traced to the child's ambivalent emotions, coming and going before the child can deal with them successfully or understand them fully.

Think about a ten-year-old boy. He has reached the point in his life when he understands that "boys don't cry when they don't get their way." He notices his friends don't cry when they strike out in baseball or when the teacher disciplines them at school. He doesn't want to cry in front of his friends. But because of all the emotional turmoil going on inside of him, often he bursts out in tears for seemingly no reason—at least no discernible reason.

Can you see how frustrating this would be for the boy? Isn't it easy to understand why he would quit situations early before the tears are likely to come?

These normal emotions will be very frustrating to the child in elementary school.

The elementary-age child may experience increased aggressiveness and possessiveness. The aggression may appear openly in fits of temper, hyperactivity, and rebellion. Or it may occur passively in immobilized stubbornness or refusal to accept things or situations. The possessiveness may be with belongings and time, or it may cause the child to withdraw and be very possessive of the giving of himself to others in relationships.

The Teenager

Teens often do one of two things in dealing with the loss of a parent. Either they drop out of everything, withdrawing from activities and people and isolating themselves behind the earphones of their CD player, or they become overinvolved in all sorts of extracurricular activities and events.

Both are attempts to run away from their troubles. Teens already are dealing with so many adjustments that to add the crisis of divorce is just about too much for a teen to manage. So they choose not to face it until they mature enough to handle the negative stresses of that crisis.

There are hazards for the teen who withdraws. While this is normal behavior, it can become abnormal and damaging if not dealt with as soon as possible. It can cause plummeting grades or misconduct at school, either of which may cause the teen to feel like dropping out. This decision may seem right at the time, but it will, of course, have lifelong repercussions. The withdrawing teen will isolate himself from social situations and relationships. Again, this is normal behavior but it leaves behind any support system, those most likely to help the teen deal with emotional stress. As such withdrawal continues, the emotions are isolated and intensified even more. They can lead the teen to self-destructive methods of coping. The teen suicide rate is highest among teens whose parents have divorced.

The overinvolved teen meets a different set of hazards. It should be remembered that this overinvolvement comes not from a curious, energetic desire to grow and experience life, but from a driving need to avoid what is causing pain.

That drive will cause the teen to enter all the extracurricular activities that school or church has to offer. Then when there are no more worthwhile, "good" activities, that teen will get involved in detrimental, destructive activities. Today's communities are filled with that kind of adolescent restlessness.

Teens often become obsessive or compulsive. The teen can be obsessed with anything, from clean hair to dirty heroes. The obsessiveness comes from a need to avoid the pain within, so, again, it drives the teen's energies and emotions. From the compulsive need to keep a room clean to the more complex compulsions that pull a teen into an addictive life-style, the resultant activities seem to temporarily remove the pain of loss from that teen's mind.

The teen in crisis will often display anger and intolerance. Although these are normal emotions, they can get a grip on a teenager's life.

Think about the reactions of your children to their divorce experience. List your children by name and age. Then determine what their crisis symptoms have been.

Name   Age

The age-level symptoms my child has exhibited:

How long has it been since the crisis occurred?

133

How do you feel your child is coping with these symptoms?

Have these symptoms heightened or diminished since the crisis?

What symptoms are causing your children the most difficulty?

What symptoms are causing you the most concern in your childrens' recovery?

What improvements have your children made in these areas since the crisis occurred?

Normal Responses of Children

Over one million kids are affected by divorce each year. And each of them will have many different reactions to their stress. Most of these reactions can be categorized into several symptomatic responses. Let us look at these normal ways children respond to crises.

Guilt

During the eighteen or more years that my husband and I have been involved with ministry to children of divorce we have seen thousands of children. If there is one response I have identified in every one of these children, it is the guilt each child assumes for the crisis.

As adults and parents we don't understand how our children can feel guilty about a decision they had no part in making and no control over. But rational or not, each child does feel the guilt of the crisis.

I felt guilt! My parents divorced when I was fourteen, old enough to understand I had nothing to do with the decision. Yet I felt as though something I had done (or not done) had contributed to their divorce.

I heard the story of a little girl whose parents had divorced. One day the little girl found her mother crying. Quickly she hurried outside, picked up something from the ground, and came back in to her mother. "Here, Mommy," she said to her mother, "here's a rock you can frow at me!"

You may be able to understand this response a little better by remembering when you were a child. Were you disciplined by your parents? Did you ever wish that something bad would happen to them so they couldn't spank you anymore?

I did. I was raised in a Christian home and taught the power of prayer. My mother spanked me with a lilac switch that she sent me to pick. Just like a child, I thought the smaller the switch the less it would hurt. Many nights I went to bed praying that one of two things would happen: Either the lilac bush would burn up overnight, or my mother would break her arm.

The bush still stands and my mother never broke her arm. But she and my father did divorce. Somehow I felt my nasty thoughts about her discipline contributed to her frustration and inability to cope with the marriage. I think that is true for every child. When something bad happens—guilt creeps in.

Another reason children struggle with guilt is because they believe their parents are strong, able to cope with anything that happens. If the little boy down the street picks on you, you just run home and get Daddy to go pick on that mean little boy's daddy and straighten out that family. If the teacher loads you with too much homework, you get Mom to go and explain things to the teacher and she lightens the homework assignments.

But what if something happens that parents can't handle? Their children think that the disaster must somehow be their fault. It's not rational—but it's the way many children think.

Perhaps the best way we can help our children overcome their guilty feelings is by consistently reaffirming to them that they did not contribute in any way to the decision to divorce. Nothing they could have done (or not done) would have changed that decision.

135

How have your children struggled with guilt?

How have you helped them to overcome that guilt?

Physical Illness

As adults we are just beginning to understand what effect emotional stress has on our physical bodies. There is a test that assigns a numerical value to various events in a person's life (e.g., a vacation, a job change, a move). Based on the previous eighteen months of one's life, the total measures the amount of stress a person is dealing with. For a very normal (if there is such a thing) divorce, without custody battles and harsh feelings, the numerical factor equals more than 300 points. The stress test indicates that anyone with more than 300 points is susceptible to a major illness within a period of months. Is it any wonder we adults feel physically sick during intense emotional stress?

The same thing is true of our children. The physical reactions we have to stress are the same ones our children have. Yet so many times we discount these physical symptoms in our children.

I know I do. I go by the "cool touch" rule. If my child's forehead is cool to the touch, he goes to school even if he claims to have a fever.

Many times a child will wake up in the morning and say to a parent, "Mommy, I've got a real bad tummy ache. Can I stay home from school?"

Often our first response is, "I can't stay home with you today. You will be fine; just get up and get moving."

More serious physical symptoms may persist, such as headaches, ulcers, respiratory illness, and allergies or asthma.

136

We need to be tuned in to our children's physical distresses. We can at least offer the nurture and physical affection they need to help them through these emotional turmoils.

What physical symptoms has your child exhibited?

Have you associated that physical distress with any emotional stress in your child? In other words, can you see a correlation between the two?

Is your child experiencing more physical illness since the crisis? Could there be a connection with their emotions?

Indifference

There are two levels of indifference that the child of divorce may exhibit. The first is a pretense that all is well. You know the child is pretending, the child recognizes the pretense, yet it is a coping mechanism to help the child deal with the negatives of the situation. It is a way to protect one's self from more hurt.

I remember a thirteen-year-old girl I met at a seminar. Her mother had forced her to attend our children's seminar. She did not want to be there. Every look, every bit of body language, and every word she spoke told me that, as we began the workshop. It was an all-day seminar and throughout the day this girl refused to participate. She sat in the back with her arms folded belligerently in front of her. She would not participate in any of the activities and refused to open her workbook or communicate in any way.

The final activity of the day was puppet therapy. I put a

bunch of puppets on the floor in front of me and told the children we were going to write a play about divorce. It would have three acts: One taking place one year before the divorce, the second at the time of the divorce, and the third a year after the divorce. The children were to produce the play, act it out, and prepare to perform it for their parents as a final activity.

The time came to choose a puppet. All at once this thirteen-year-old elbowed her way to the front and made a mad dive for my favorite puppet. It was a big monkey with long arms that wrap around your neck, and a look that begs to be loved.

She picked up the monkey, hugged it close to her, and went to her spot in the back of the room. We worked on the play without her, and presented it to the parents as they joined us.

Finally it was time for us to clean up and go home. This girl still had no intention of letting go of the monkey. I realized this might be a divinely prepared opportunity to confront the real issues bothering her. So I walked up to her and said, "You are going to have to give me back my puppet now."

For a long moment she stood there hugging the puppet. Tears came to her eyes and began to run down her face. Finally with great emotion she thrust it into my hands, exclaiming, "Take it—it just wanted to be loved!" Then she turned to run. I stopped her and gave her a big bear hug. She didn't want to be there in my arms. She struggled to get loose and when she couldn't, she stood there, for what seemed a very long time, just motionless and stiff. I whispered in her ear, "You're the one who wants to be loved, aren't you?" The dam burst and she began crying loud wracking sobs. Her arms went around my neck and grabbed until I was the one who could not get loose.

The door of her pretense had opened. Finally she was ready for some intervention to set her on the road to recovery. I counseled her and her mother briefly, and then left them in the care of the singles pastor at that church and returned home to Chicago. Months later, the pastor wrote to tell me what a wonderful transformation had taken place in that hurting young girl's life.

The second form of indifference is more difficult to recognize. It is a subtle not-caring attitude. You don't see any pretense in the attitude because, in fact, the child is not pretending. The hurt is buried deep within—too deep for the child to deal with, and an attitude of indifference exists regarding the divorce experience.

A danger exists with this form of indifference. Children who cease to care about family matters are the children that can easily cease to care about themselves. This attitude can permeate every aspect of such a child's life and tragically ruin opportunities to become all that God wants for the child.

A few years ago, we were preparing a video on our ministry to divorced families. On the tape, I interviewed several of the children who had been through our program. One of them was a young girl about eleven years old whose parents had divorced eight years previously, and who never saw her father. I asked her, "How do you feel about your parents' divorce?"

"Oh, I don't mind," she responded. "I never knew my dad and I don't miss him. My mom and I and my sister and brother are getting along just fine."

Later I interviewed these same children again. This time I used a more nonthreatening approach. I asked: "How do you think children feel when their parents divorce and they don't get to see one of their parents anymore?"

This time the same eleven-year-old quickly responded with great emotion. "I think they feel so bad they wish they were dead!"

She did not even realize she felt that way, the root of rejection and hurt was buried so deep under her facade of indifference.

Do your children pretend that they feel better about the crisis than what you as a parent perceive they feel?

How do they carry on this pretense?

Have you recognized the existence of a pervading indifference in your children's lives?

When questioned do your children fail to exhibit hurt?

The Reconciliation Fantasy

With respect to the fantasy of reconciliation, I feel it is very important to make this statement first: If there is *any possibility* at all for you and your former spouse to work out your differences and reconcile, *you need to put all your energies toward that goal!*

Most of the children our ministry touches have a dream that their parents will get back together. It persists long after all actual possibilities of reconciliation have faded.

This is a response I have recognized in myself. My parents were divorced twenty-five years before my mother died. Two years after her death, my dad died. My first thought as I stood at my father's casket was this: *Well, maybe God will put them in mansions side by side up in heaven!*

I have seen many strange and humorous scenarios take place as children attempt to reunite their parents. Some have been quite sober! My husband had a little boy come in for counseling. His prayer request—"Pastor Jim, will you pray that God will kill that man living with my mom so Dad can come home?" The "man" was a stepfather who had married the boy's mother two years earlier.

A little girl I know who lived with her father told him she was preparing a very special dinner for just him and herself. The father planned to be home early that evening for this special time with his daughter. At the same time, she told her mother (who lived in the same city) that her father would be gone that night, and invited her mother over for dinner. Her father came home and went upstairs to clean up. Her mother arrived and the girl exited out the back door. Dinner was ready with candles on the table, music playing, and all the atmosphere she thought necessary to convince her parents to get married again.

We need to allow our children the right to their hopes and dreams, but we also need to reassert the reality of our situation, such as, "Honey, I know you want us to get back together again, but it just isn't possible. I am sorry this happened to our family but I am moving forward in my life. I want you to do that too. I'll do anything I can to help you. We both love you very much, but we can never be a family again."

140

How has your child struggled with a desire to reconcile the family?

How have you been able to help your child overcome this struggle?

Have you consistently reasserted the reality of your situation without making your child feel wrong for wanting her dreams to come true?

Hatred for Parents

It is most difficult for a parent to understand hatred coming from a child, particularly if that parent is struggling with guilty feelings about divorce. Yet expressing hatred for a parent is a child's normal response to the negative emotional fallout of divorce.

The hatred most often will be expressed toward the custodial parent. After all, this parent bears the majority of responsibility for the family. The demands on time, emotional and physical energies, and finances are almost insurmountable. There just isn't time to sit down and read stories together anymore. There just isn't an extra thirty dollars for a new pair of tennis shoes.

Hatred may be expressed for the parent who has left the home. "I hate my dad for leaving me and I hope I never have to see him again" is often the response from a hurting, rejected, love-starved child.

To successfully deal with these outbursts we have to understand deep hurt and be able to hear expressed hatred without taking offense. Rarely is real hatred underneath all the outward expression. To the contrary, there is the confusion, loneliness, and frustration of being trapped in a situation that seems to be changing everything in life. Responding with calm, consistent love will thwart hatred's expression and lead to a more positive way of dealing with those frustrations.

Hatred can be an insidious force in your child's life. It moves him back to guilt and paralyzed emotions, rather than forward to positive adjustment. Reaffirm your love for your child. Gently and consistently lead him to an ability to give and receive love.

Has your child ever expressed hatred toward you?

What was your response?

Think about a time when your child was dealing with expressed hatred. What circumstances could have been causing the frustration your child was feeling?

Has your child expressed hatred toward the parent who is gone? How does that make you feel?

A child needs the love of both his parents. How can you separate your feelings of rejection and resentment toward your former spouse and encourage your child to develop love and understanding toward his other parent?

In this chapter we have looked closely at what children face when their parents divorce. It's been a hard chapter. Perhaps it has caused you great distress. But it is necessary to understand the negatives in order to move ahead to positive adjustment to a crisis.

The real challenge facing parents regarding their child is this: You can bring alive only an outlook that is authentic for you. The actual words you use are less important than the attitude you convey about your situation. The real challenge then for you—making peace with divorce yourself. Learn to move forward out of yesterday toward tomorrow.

Matthew 18:2,5–6 gives us some good advice: "He [Jesus] called a small child over and had him stand among them. . . . 'And whoever welcomes a little child like this . . . welcomes me. But if anyone causes one of these little ones who believe in me to sin, it would be better for him to have a large millstone hung around his neck and to be drowned in the depths of the sea.'"

I challenge you to educate yourself all you can about your child's specific needs as a result of the crisis of divorce. Then add to this knowledge your own personal insights.

Design your own recovery techniques for your family. The time you invest in this kind of creative recovery will move you way up the ladder of positive adjustment and out of the devastation of divorce. By turning in a positive direction, growth can begin for everyone; there can emerge a closeness and depth of understanding never before achieved.

Remember the illustration of Jesus and His disciples during the storm on the Sea of Galilee. Let Jesus' words be an inspiration to you: "Let us go to the other side!"

10

Single and Parenting

Chapter Focus

God desires to use you to help your children work through the experience of your divorce. You as a parent can become the hero your children need to set them free from the bondage of divorce distress.

What God's Word Says

"See to it that no one misses the grace of God and that no bitter root grows up to cause trouble and defile many" (Hebrews 12:15).

Vignette

The enemy had captured and carried her away from friends and family. After leaving her alone for hours of frightening captivity while they deliberated her fate, the enemy finally came to get her.

They tied her to a stake, blindfolded her, and spread straw around her feet. Then the enemy gathered around chanting and wildly dancing to the eerie beat of drums. Suddenly all grew quiet. The stillness was excruciating as she wondered what the enemy was doing. All at once she heard a crackling sound and smelled the scent of burning straw.

Frightened, she began to scream for help. The flames grew hotter and hotter.

All at once she heard the sound of horse's hooves, and someone called her name. She felt strong hands cut her bonds and lift her away from the flames. As the blindfold was removed, she saw him, and, with a gasp of relief, said, "You came just in time."

That scenario took place in my backyard when I was a kid. Lots of childhood friends and I acted out our imaginings.

What part does imagination play with children of divorce? Imagine with me the feeling of that child, bound by a force greater than she, with destruction inching its way closer with every agonizing moment.

Now, while you are still in the midst of your imaginings, look at the following paragraph from *Surviving the Breakup* by Wallterstein and Kelly:

> For children and adolescents, the separation and its aftermath was the most stressful period of their lives. The family rupture evoked an acute sense of shock, intense fears, and grieving which the children may find overwhelming. . . . Adding significantly to the widespread distress of the children is the fact that many of them face the tensions and sorrows of divorce with little help from their parents, or anyone else, for during the critical months following the separation, parental care often diminishes, not because parents are necessarily less loving or less concerned with their children during divorce, but because the radical alterations in their lives tend to focus their attention on their own troubles.

I believe the pressures these children deal with call up the same sense of helplessness that the girl at the stake felt. These children plead to be rescued and wait for their hero to come, remove their blinders, and set them free. They long to be able to say: "You came just in time."

Do you sense any distress in your children?

> What concerns do you have regarding their ability to cope
> with your divorce?

I remember the distress I felt; I was fourteen years old when my parents divorced. They were active Christians in the little rural community church where they had been raised. But their twenty-five-year marriage did not survive the emotional upheaval caused by my mother's menopausal experience.

My parents were devastated by this development. They felt that a failure to live according to God's laws had removed them from His favor. They were unable to prepare my sister or me in any way for the changes the divorce would bring.

The night my father left, I did not know whether he meant he was leaving for a trip out of town or forever. In the weeks and months to come I would be isolated by my hurt, having no one to reach out to me with healing. I felt as though I had been trapped in a nightmare.

The small, conservative church we attended was unable to accept this breach of conduct from two of its stalwarts. We were asked to leave the congregation. We left and never returned.

The "bitter root" of Hebrews 12:15 began to grow up "to cause trouble and defile" me because of my parents' divorce. It would be several years before I learned to understand its effect on my life and become capable of eradicating the "bitter root."

There are more than sixteen million children right now in the United States who are living in one-parent homes. Many thousands of those children feel as helpless as if they were blindfolded and tied to a stake.

Parents who have taken their families through divorce find it difficult to deal with their children's resultant negative emotions. It makes us feel so much more responsible for their hurt when we acknowledge its depth. The guilt can paralyze us, so that we are unable to help our child overcome the destructiveness.

Let me give you one more quotation from *Surviving the Breakup:*

> We have reported as widespread a diminished capacity to parent at the time of the family breakup which, while often temporary, may have long-lasting implication and may significantly affect the coping capacities of both children and adolescents and the perseverance of symptomatic behaviors and distressed feelings.
>
> Put simply, the central hazard which divorce poses to the psychological health and development of children and adolescents is in the diminished or disrupted parenting which so often follows in the wake of the rupture and which can become consolidated within the post-divorce family.

That brings us to the purpose of this chapter. Having recognized the reality of the negative experience of divorce in our kid's lives, we want to begin moving up the ladder of recovery to positive and successful parenting and child rearing.

What positive changes would you like to see in each of your children's lives?

There is a single-parent story in the Bible that can help point the way for us.

Remember—God can and does heal the hurts of a divorce experience in our children's lives. God cares about our children infinitely more than we do. The words of His Son should give us hope: "Let the little children come to me."

Let's take a look at our single parent in the Bible and see

what we can learn from her example. The story is of Hagar and Ishmael. This biblical single-parent family underwent some negative experiences in their lives. Yet God's unconditional love for them is evident.

Read Genesis 21:14–20:

> Early the next morning Abraham took some food and a skin of water and gave them to Hagar. He set them on her shoulders and then sent her off with the boy. She went on her way and wandered in the desert of Beersheba.
>
> When the water in the skin was gone, she put the boy under one of the bushes. Then she went off and sat down nearby, about a bowshot away, for she thought, "I cannot watch the boy die." And as she sat there nearby, she began to sob.
>
> God heard the boy crying, and the angel of God called to Hagar from heaven and said to her, "What is the matter, Hagar? Do not be afraid; God has heard the boy crying as he lies there. Lift the boy up and take him by the hand, for I will make him into a great nation."
>
> Then God opened her eyes and she saw a well of water. So she went and filled the skin with water and gave the boy a drink. God was with the boy as he grew up.

Several realities of parenting after a crisis are included in these verses. Understanding what can happen can move us from our paralyzing fears and doubts about our children's adjustment to the point of reaching them where they hurt most, becoming the "hero" who comes "just in time." We can become successful single parents as God intends. In the rest of this chapter we will see how what happened in Hagar's life can happen in ours.

The Discouragement of Failure

Recognizing the child's hurt may have a self-absorbing effect on the parent rather than a unifying effect on the remaining family unit. Notice the example of Hagar and Ishmael. They had been cast out of their home with Abraham. Although they had set out for a new life, they had few provisions. And as they moved farther and farther into the unknown, those provisions began to dwindle. Finally, miles from where they used to live, and miles from where they wanted to be, they found themselves in the midst of the desert. They were alone, hungry, and tired, their provisions all gone. Their strength was gone, and with it their hope.

The son was looking to his mother for help, but she had no more to give. She recognized the severity of their circumstances. She had failed; she could no longer be to her son what every natural instinct told her she should be. In the middle of the desert, hungry, hopeless, and guilt-ridden, she lay down her son, fully anticipating his death. Not realizing she might yet comfort him with her presence if not with food, and unable to bear his dying, she tried to get out of earshot of his cries.

That's the way it is with many single-parent families—the "diminished" parenting "in the wake of the rupture," the parents' "attention on their own troubles."

We don't like to recognize such parental failure—the knowledge of which hits right in the middle of our guilt-ridden fears. Crises can pull a family unit apart or bring it closer together. Recognition of the negative possibility can become the catalyst to move us toward the positive possibility of becoming closer. Hagar didn't turn her back on Ishmael because she didn't love him. She could bear neither to see his pain nor to feel her own.

Think back to the onset of the crisis in your life. At the time your family unit broke apart did you feel as Hagar felt?

What "provisions" did you recognize were becoming used up as you entered the unknown experience beyond the crisis?

Did you reach a moment when you almost lost hope during your desert experience? Describe your feelings.

149

The Isolation of Grief

When both parent and child are grieving, that grief will isolate them from each other. This extends the self-absorbing effect of a crisis throughout the grieving process. Although a normal tendency, it has this hazard: Instead of the remaining family members finding a way to pull back together and restructure after the crisis, they go through the grieving process isolated from each other. This creates the environment for disjointed family living.

Many single-parent families struggle with becoming a family unit again. A family long past the time of their crisis may seem to be recovered and moving on with their lives, but without exhibiting any real cohesiveness as a family. Everyone seems to be living separate lives. Each dwells side by side in the same house but never work together as a family unit. This was true of Hagar and Ishmael. She was grieving in her own isolated corner of the desert, and he in his.

In what ways are the members of your family pulling together and becoming a cohesive family unit since your family crisis?

In what ways do you recognize that your family members are isolated in their grieving, making separate adjustments toward healing, rather than as a family?

Healing for the Child

God desires to use the parent as the tool of healing for the child. See how God intervened in the experience of Hagar and Ishmael. Both were alone and sobbing in the desert. But "God heard the boy crying" (Genesis 21:17).

That does not necessarily mean our children's needs are more important than our own in times of crisis. Just as in times of joy and contentment God blesses the family from parent to child, so in times of sorrow and destruction God intervenes in a family from parent to child. I believe that is God's plan for parenthood.

What is it that was hurting Hagar the most? Wasn't it her sense of parental failure, her feeling that she could no longer be to her son what her every natural instinct told her she should be?

God recognized her pain and knew the solution lay in showing her how to become again what she longed to be—the source of nurture.

God heard both mother and child sobbing there in that desert. He could have sent a ministering angel to Ishmael and restored him. But that wouldn't have ministered to Hagar. So God restored her belief that she could be the mother her son needed most: "'Lift the boy up and take him by the hand'" (v. 18).

I have seen single parents so paralyzed by fears that they can no longer be effective, willing to abdicate their responsibility to someone else. That is not God's design for parenthood.

Read Psalm 139:16: "All the days ordained for me were written in your book before one of them came to be."

That verse has a powerful message for single parents. God knew every moment and every circumstance of your life before you were conceived. He knew every moment and circumstance of your child's life before conception. In His wisdom, He decided you were the best possible person to raise the children He gave to you. He knew in advance every situation you would face.

In what ways have you felt inadequate as a parent to help your child overcome the destruction of your divorce?

151

List the ways God has used you to help your child overcome the negative effects of your divorce.

Healing for the Parent

As the parent becomes a source of healing for the child, the parent will find healing. The angel of God said to Hagar: "What is the matter, Hagar? Do not be afraid; God has heard the boy crying as he lies there. Lift the boy up and take him by the hand, for I will make him into a great nation" (Genesis 21:17–18).

God gave this single mother her focus back. He made her an effective parent again. He moved her forward out of her grief and gave her a way to solidify the family unit. From that point on, there is no further indication of Hagar sobbing. By knowing how to heal her son, she achieved healing herself.

I think of the example of a single parent mother and her daughter that I know. The parents divorced when Traci was only eighteen months old. Traci and her mother entered our divorce recovery workshops when Traci was twelve years old.

Her mother said to me, "For some reason I always felt, from the day of the divorce, the person who would be least affected in this family was my youngest daughter, Traci. I thought because she was only eighteen months old, and never really had the chance to know her father, that she would not care about the breakup."

During the sixth week of the workshops, Traci came to her mother and said, "Mom, I want to sing a song to you that I wrote."

This is Traci's song.

> Sometimes things happen we can't foresee,
>   And they seem too big for me.
> Then my heart feels cracked in two,
>   but God always knows just what to do.

152

Just look around and what do you see?
It's God's great big family.
What's minus one, when you can have
a ton of family?

It's a crack in half that's been put
Back together again,
Put back with God.

—Traci McMeans, 1986

When Traci finished, her mother asked, "What's the 'crack in half?'"

Traci replied, "Mommy, it was my heart!"

For the first time her mother realized how deeply Traci had been hurt by the divorce. "I cried in gratefulness that God had seen her need, and He had been able to do something about it even when I couldn't," she recalled.

What kind of healing do you want to help your child achieve?

How would seeing your child recover in this way help you find healing for yourself?

Direction from God

God alone will understand the specific priority need of your child. He will open your eyes to see that need. Do you remember the nursery rhyme about the old woman in the shoe?

153

There was an old woman who lived in a shoe.
She had so many children, she didn't know what to do.
She gave them some broth, without any bread,
She whipped them all soundly, and sent them to bed.

A vast number of single parents identify with the old woman in the shoe. They live in "shoe box" apartments, too crowded for their family yet all they can afford. And I've been in many single-parent homes where there was no more than "some broth, without any bread." Financial distress is a common occurrence among single parents. And for the single-parent breadwinner, overworked and emotionally-drained, sometimes just one child can seem like "so many children, she doesn't know what to do."

As a result, whether or not a child is "whipped soundly and sent to bed" may very well depend on the single parent's emotional reserve at the end of the day rather than on the behavior of the kids. For there is no more blessed time of the day than the first few quiet moments immediately following the children's bedtime.

How could the old woman in the shoe know what the important needs of the family were? Did they need a bigger shoe, more money, fewer family members, more food, better discipline, more private time for Mom, or what? What was the *greatest need?*

What was Hagar's greatest need—or Ishmael's? Hagar obviously didn't know. But God did! Ishmael had two crucial needs: First he needed a drink of water. More than a soft bed, a meal, a home, a camel to ride on, or a father to be with, at that moment, one of his greatest needs was for a drink of water. Instead of sending an angel to give him a drink, God "opened her [Hagar's] eyes and she saw a well of water" (Genesis 21:19). God knew Ishmael's immediate need and, furthermore, directed his mother in meeting it. He will do the same for you.

Ishmael's second crucial need was the nurturing touch of his mother. God said, "Lift the boy up and take him by the hand" (v. 18). God saw his need, and helped Hagar become a nurturing, effective parent once again.

In *Children of Divorce,* Louise Despert points out: "It is not divorce, but the emotional situation in the home, with or with-

154

out divorce, that is the determining factor in a child's adjustment. A child is very disturbed when the relationship between his parents is very disturbed."

As we allow God to show us the crucial needs of our children, He will inspire us with verses like Isaiah 43:19: "See, I am doing a new thing! Now it springs up; do you not perceive it?" And Psalm 127:1: "Unless the Lord builds the house, its builders labor in vain."

With God's help, determine the significant needs of your children.

How can you become the tool of healing to help them achieve recovery?

Spiritual Development

Through the parent, the child will recognize God's presence. God didn't say to Ishmael: "I will make you into a great nation; I will be with you as you grow up." He said it to the mother! He gave her the responsibility to nurture and instruct her son spiritually so he could feel and sense God's presence in his life. Unfortunately, Scripture implies that Hagar wasn't completely effective in her spiritual responsibility, for Ishmael did not have a godly impact as an adult.

Christian parents—even divorced ones—have a biblical responsibility to educate, cultivate, and nurture their children until they reach maturity. They need "an authority figure. If parents do not provide the needed leadership, their children will seek it elsewhere. Without firm leadership in the home, children

will find someone outside the family who will tell them what to do. Children desperately need someone whom they can follow and to whom they can give their allegiance. . . . They will find a replacement if the parents abdicate their position."
Deuteronomy states the principle in 6:6–9.

> These commandments that I give you today are to be upon your hearts. Impress them on your children. Talk about them when you sit at home and when you walk along the road, when you lie down and when you get up. Tie them as symbols on your hands and bind them on your foreheads. Write them on the doorframes of your houses and on your gates.

God has given us as parents the responsibility for our children's spiritual development. We must recognize that our child will learn to experience God's presence through us. In the next chapter we will explore ways to do this.

> How are you helping your children to recognize God's presence in their lives?

Just as your child is a unique gift to you from God, he or she also has a unique set of needs that only you and God together can meet. You can be the tool of healing for your child as God moves you into that child's area of hurt. Jesus loves you—and your children; He wants your family to be whole. You can be a living, breathing, cohesive family unit that lights the way to wholeness for broken lives around you.

> Jesus loves the little children
> Who have faced their parents' divorce.
> Hurt, rejected, lonely, tough;
> Jesus' love is quite enough.
> Jesus loves the little children of divorce.
> —Barbara Dycus, 1993

11

Developing Your Family's Spiritual Life

Chapter Focus

The lives of people whose families have come apart resemble a crazy quilt. Each piece—each experience—may seem like a meaningless fragment, without design. Yet as the pieces are put together in the framework of God's grace and power, a work of art emerges. Wholeness replaces brokenness, worth replaces worthlessness, and beauty replaces ugliness.

What God's Word Says

"There is a time for everything, and a season for every activity under heaven: a time to be born and a time to die, a time to plant and a time to uproot, a time to kill and a time to heal, a time to tear down and a time to build, a time to weep and a time to laugh, a time to mourn and a time to dance, a time to scatter stones and a time to gather them, a time to embrace and a time to refrain, a time to search and a time to give up, a time to keep and a time to throw away, a time to tear and a time to mend, a time to be silent and a time to speak, a time to love and a time to hate, a time for war and a time for peace" (Ecclesiastes 3:1–8).

Vignette

One of my treasured possessions is a crazy quilt made by my

157

great-grandmother. It is truly a work of art, made from swatches of wool and velvet, beautifully embroidered with designs and flowers. My grandmother passed the quilt down to my mother. When Jim and I married, my mother passed it on to me. With the quilt, she passed its history.

Each swatch tells a story. One piece of fabric, for example, came from my great-grandfather's wedding suit, another from his burial suit. Another piece came from my great-grandmother's wedding dress, and still another from the burial dress of their two-year-old daughter who died of smallpox.

That quilt is much more than a thing of beauty. It is a record of a family's daily struggles and joys. Created from the pieces of life's experiences, many of them symbolizing broken hopes and unfulfilled dreams, it became much more. Each swatch, when pieced together by the skillful hands of my great-grandmother, became a part of something much more beautiful than it originally had been. Then as she finished with beautifully embroidered flowers and designs, the remnants became works of art. The lives of people who have undergone a breakdown in their family are like that crazy quilt.

I am somewhat of a collector. And although I don't have any Van Gogh or Renoir paintings, I do have my great-grandmother's watch, my dad's baby plate, and my mother's apple peeler. These and other such things have become a part of me.

When we moved to Florida from Chicago many of my antiques seemed out of place in Florida's tropical decorating schemes. So I began to dispose of some of my collection. One of the things I thought I wanted to get rid of is an English secretary desk (from which I still write). One day an antique dealer came to my home and haggled with me about the desk. He made a comment that has repeated itself many times in my mind: "Nothing has a value. Everything has a price."

For me, those words were emotionally charged. It is impossible for me to reduce my belief that these antiques are valuable because of who they belonged to instead of how much I can get for them.

Yet that comment has great significance to me for another

reason. God's Word tells me that I "have been bought and paid for by Christ, so [I] belong to him" (1 Corinthians 7:23, *Living Bible*). It also says that I am "more valuable to him than many sparrows" (Matthew 10:31, *Living Bible*). God saw my value, and He was willing to pay the price to redeem me.

God has placed a high value on people, and that includes the single-parent family. They may be scarred and broken, but to God they are priceless. That's why it is so important to help the single-parent family learn to reach the future God has for it. Stating the principles will not be enough. The principles must be applied.

Velma Carter and Lynn Leavenworth, in counseling thousands of families, observed a difference between what those families confessed in church and how they related that to life in the home: "Few of them appear to have experience in relating the articles of their faith to the major decisions and shaping experiences of their lives." They concluded: "In the personal discovery of basic religious faith, the beleaguered parent finds the foundation for building hope and love, and in the process he or she develops a framework for coping."

By developing a plan for your family's spiritual life, you as a single parent will be giving your family a framework for coping with their negative experiences.

What are the spiritual goals that you have already determined will help your family make a positive adjustment to their crisis?

Ecclesiastes 3:1–8 captures the single-parent experience. It shows that life is full of changes both good and bad, and that we are passing continuously through these changes. Solomon states at the beginning of these verses: "To everything there is a season." You are in the season of parenting as a single.

I remember living in the north during the winter. Many years I wondered if that season would ever end. Now, living in Florida, I wonder the same about the summers. Maybe you are wondering about your season of single parenting—will it ever end? The important thing to remember is that a season is just one segment of a whole. God desires us to be spiritually equipped and ready to be whole, not segmented into "seasonal living." But that will take some planning. My husband Jim has a favorite saying, "Plan the work and work the plan."

For the single-parent family, knowledge that God watches every season of our lives and can make sense of the changes brought about by each will be the foundation for learning to cope with these changes.

Ecclesiastes 3:1–11 will be the road map for this chapter and for the single-parent family to develop a spiritual family life. Much of the responsibility for this growth will be placed on the single parent. God wants the parent to be the tool of recovery and growth for the entire family.

Let's consider some of the biblical principles for spiritual growth in Ecclesiastes 3.

A Time to be Born

The language of this verse implies offspring, family.

In Psalm 127:3 we read that our children are a "heritage" from the Lord, a "reward" from Him (KJV). Our children are gifts from God. We need to understand the value of the gift in both the eyes of the giver and the receiver.

God loves to give gifts to His people. His gifts are never intended to bring harm, trouble, or sorrow to His people. He gives His gifts to enrich our lives and to make us better than we would have been without the gift.

Matthew 7:11 explains this in terms that we as parents can understand: "If you, then, though you are evil, know how to give good gifts to your children, how much more will your Father in heaven give good gifts to those who ask him?"

Many single parents struggle with the demands of single parenting. Many feel inadequate to raise their children. Some Christian single parents feel inundated with the demands of parenting and consider turning over the nurturing of those little lives to the non-Christian parent.

God wants you to understand that His good gift of that precious child was good before the season of loss, through the season it remains good, and long after the season is over, the value of that good gift will go on enriching the family's life.

A Time to Die

Just as God decided the exact moment in time when each life would begin, so He has determined when that life will end: "From one man he made every nation of men, that they should inhabit the whole earth; and he determined the times set for them and the exact places where they should live" (Acts 17:26).

How comforting these two revelations about life and death can be to the single-parent family. To grasp God's perspective on loss, to recognize that this season cannot alter His divine purposes in the lives of our family members as we allow His plan to unfold, is a life-changing discovery.

A Time to Plant

Parents have a responsibility to educate and nurture a child until that child reaches maturity. Deuteronomy 6:6–9 states it clearly:

> These commandments that I give you today are to be upon your hearts. Impress them on your children. Talk about them when you sit at home and when you walk along the road, when you lie down and when you get up. Tie them as symbols on your hands and bind them on your foreheads. Write them on the doorframes of your houses and on your gates.

We are to instill God's principles in the lives of our children so they might have the foundation they need to become mature, fully-functioning adults. Listen to the words of Psalm 78:2–6:

> I will utter things from of old—what we have heard and known, what our fathers have told us. We will not hide them from their children; we will tell the next generation the praiseworthy deeds of the Lord, his power, and the wonders he has done. He decreed statutes for Jacob and established the law in Israel, which he commanded our forefathers to teach their children, so the next

generation would know them, even the children yet to be born, and they in turn would tell their children.

A Time to Pluck Up

"Uproot" can be defined this way:
"To pluck up, to tear up by the roots or from the foundation; to eradicate, to exterminate; to destroy."

Divorce brings a plucking up, a tearing apart at the roots, that will threaten the family members with instability and distress. In the postcrisis single-parent family this stability must be reaffirmed.

> God has established the institution of the parent as one of His ruling authorities on earth. To this position has been delegated both the right to rule children and all the power necessary to succeed in training children according to God's plan. This position is the direct agency through which children are to receive ruling during their childhood. That is, it is through this position that each child is to receive protection, direction and instruction.

Children are devastated by divorce because God's principle for their nurture has been broken. The single parent must understand this. Recovery from divorce cannot be achieved by adapting to external changes only. Nor will reaching positive responses to negative emotions bring the family into full recovery.

Full recovery will be achieved when the child is back within the protection of a parent who is following God's principles for that family. Single parents must deal with this spiritual issue and commit their lives through the grace of God to the biblical principle of training their child according to God's plan.

In light of these first four principles in Ecclesiastes, define your role of spiritual responsibility to your children.

A Time to Kill

This time can help the family move more quickly into recovery. Children struggle with their desire to reconcile the family long after all real hope of reconciliation has disappeared. Like the little boy who will not let go his fistful of candy to free his hand from the candy jar, so the child of divorce who will not let go his fantasy will not be free from the destructive period of his parent's divorce.

A Time to Heal

Single parents hurt! Their children hurt. They have wounds which need healing. One of the greatest therapies God ever gave to human beings is the therapy of forgiveness. Without it we would live defeated lives, held bondage by our guilt and failure. Forgiveness needs to be a consistent, continuing part of every single-parent family's spiritual life.

A Time to Tear Down

"Tear down" is a term that people in crisis understand. Divorce can stretch the parent and child to the breaking point. The biblical principles that overcome emotional stress need to be incorporated into daily life in the home.

A Time to Build

It is time for new life to be constructed. The Master Architect has the plans ready. The single-parent family is ready to invest its very life in the construction process.

The church is the rebuilder—the construction company for the single-parent family. Church life must become an integral part of single-parent family life.

Psalm 127:1 says: "Unless the Lord builds the house, its builders labor in vain." I encourage you to become involved in a good Bible-believing church. Many churches are becoming involved in the specific needs of single-parent families. You can help! And you can be helped.

A Time to Weep and Mourn

In the recovery process the single parent has two major concerns.

First, have I damaged my child permanently? By being a child of divorce, will my child be hindered from ever having a solid, lasting marriage relationship?

Second, in the spiritual realm, am I forever condemned because of my failure? Is divorce too great a sin for God to eradicate completely from my life? Does He want to rid me of its blight, or am I marked for life?

The Old Testament indicates that

> The Lord, the Lord, [is] the compassionate and gracious God, slow to anger, abounding in love and faithfulness, maintaining love to thousands, and forgiving wickedness, rebellion and sin. Yet he does not leave the guilty unpunished; he punishes the children and their children for the sin of the fathers to the third and fourth generations (Exodus 34:6–7).

These verses tells us that although God is long-suffering, has great mercy, and forgives sin, He will not clear the guilty one who chooses to remain guilty. That sin can affect that guilty person's offspring for up to four generations.

We need only to look at our world today to realize the truth of this. Alcoholism begets alcoholic children, drug abuse begets drug abusers, and rebellion begets rebellious sons and daughters. Professionals have assessed the evidence and discovered that divorce also repeats in families.

There is another link in our understanding of this truth so vital to know and pass on to those who need it.

For the guilty one who desires to repent of his guilt, the New Testament indicates that God's grace is sufficient to break the pattern of sin and remove its penalty.

Romans 5:18 points out that "just as the result of one trespass was condemnation for all men, so also the result of one act of righteousness was justification that brings life for all men." God's grace restores the guilty to favor with God. It removes the penalty of law from that guilty person. It also breaks the chain of sin within the lives of families.

I do not anticipate my son, Jimmy, will become an alcoholic or drug abuser. Nor do I expect my daughters will experience divorce just because their parents did. They will be held accountable for their sins only.

Ezekiel 18:14–32 is a portion of Scripture which we must teach to single parents who are concerned with these two questions. Read verse 20:

> The soul who sins is the one who will die. The son will not share the guilt of the father, nor will the father share the guilt of the son. The righteousness of the righteous man will be credited to him, and the wickedness of the wicked will be charged against him.

Do you think your divorce has caused permanent damage to your children? How?

What evidence have you seen that this may be true in your children?

Do you feel like "Secondhand Rose" because of your divorce?

Do you feel marked down to "bargain basement" life instead of being able to enjoy "designer living"?

How can you learn to apply this principle from Ezekiel to your fears and beliefs in these two areas?

A Time to Laugh and Dance

The knowledge that God forgives the guilty, clearing them of the penalty of that sin, ushers in a time of great joy for the single-parent family.

Our church built a new sanctuary in 1987 to seat five thousand people. In the construction process huge steel beams weighing 180 tons each were raised by gigantic cranes to rest atop the concrete pillars designed to support them. The time came for those gigantic cranes to release their support and for the pillars to stand alone. What great rejoicing there was when the cranes unhooked the beams and nothing happened! The pillars took on the weight of those beams just as they were designed to do.

Single-parent families can take on the weight of life and build successful futures.

> Therefore, since we have been justified through faith, we have peace with God through our Lord Jesus Christ, through whom we have gained access by faith into this grace in which we now stand. And we rejoice in the hope of the glory of God (Romans 5:1–2).

There is a chorus which should be heard by all children in single-parent families:

> Little children, rejoice, you're a child of the King
> Rejoice, you're a child of the King.
> Rejoice, you're a child of the King.
> Lift your head up high, rejoice, you're a child of the King.

Divorce need not burden families' lives forever and cause them to hang their heads in sorrow and pain. Through God's grace we can lift our heads up high and build a life beyond crisis.

How is your family standing strong, apart from your personal crisis?

How has God and His Word helped you to learn to bear the weight of this new life?

A Time to Scatter Stones and Gather Them

Single parents need to teach their children to use the Word of God to break down walls of negative emotions and to gather building blocks of adjustment. These positive emotional responses will build a foundation for recovery.

A Time to Embrace and a Time to Refrain

It is very important for single parents to allow themselves time to recover from the wound of a failed relationship before they try to move on to new relationships. As Bruce Fisher says in his book *Rebuilding: When Your Relationship Ends*: "I suggest you do not become involved in another long-term, committed love-relationship until you have emotionally worked through the ending of the past love-relationship."

The season of single parenting is the time to concentrate on each family member's personal relationship with Christ, and to refrain from either embracing or rebounding into unhealthy new relationships. Isaiah 54 says: "Break out into loud and joyful song, Jerusalem, for she who was abandoned has more blessings now than she whose husband stayed. For your Creator will be your 'husband' " (vv. 1,5, *Living Bible*).

A Time to Search and a Time to Give Up

Divorce is an experience that suddenly creates single-parent families, bringing confusion and change into the lives of every family member. These changes require adapting to a new lifestyle. The changes will do away with some things that have been a part of their lives for a long time. You, the parent, will need to be prepared to help your family members understand the changes and restructure their lives as God gives you direction.

Isaiah 48:17 tells you: "I am the Lord your God, who teaches you what is best for you, who directs you in the way you should go." And Proverbs 3:5–6 directs you to "trust in the Lord with all your heart and lean not on your own understanding; in all your ways acknowledge him, and he will make your paths straight."

These previous principles require a forward thrust in your family life. Think about the time which has elapsed since your family crisis. Where have you begun to move forward?

What changes are you able to list as positive?

In what areas do you feel your family is still "dragging its feet" in adjusting to a new life?

A Time to Keep and a Time to Throw Away

The changes not only will create the need to adapt to a new life-style, but also will make it necessary for the children to adapt to a new relationship with both parents.

Children of divorce have a right to both their parents. The frustrations, hostilities, and anger of the failing marriage must be thrown away for the sake of keeping vibrant, healthy, parent-child relationships with both parents whenever possible.

God's Word has much to say about good parental relationships.

168

Complete the following. First, explain how the Scripture portion supports the listed principle. Then evaluate your own home in light of these five aspects of healthy parent-child relationships.

The Home Needs an Atmosphere of Respect
Read Ephesians 6:2–3
How do you evaluate your home?

Rewards of a Good Parental Relationship
Read Proverbs 23:24–25
How do you evaluate your home?

Penalty for Bad Parental Relationships
Read Proverbs 29:15
How do you evaluate your home?

God's Promise to the Children
Read Proverbs 3:1–2
How do you evaluate your home?

God's Promise to the Parent
Read Proverbs 31:28
How do you evaluate your home?

A Time to Tear and a Time to Mend

One truth seems elementary, but needs to be repeated: Divorce is a season. Seasons have a beginning and an end. With God's help the single-parent family will put the pieces of their lives back together in a pattern of hope.

The following verse from Jeremiah can be a great encouragement.

> I will make an everlasting covenant with them, promising never again to desert them, but only to do them good. I will put a desire into their hearts to worship me, and they shall never leave me. I will rejoice to do them good and will replant them in this land, with great joy (Jeremiah 32:40–41, *Living Bible*).

A Time to be Silent and a Time to Speak

Matthew Henry comments on Ecclesiastes' "time to be silent" and "time to speak" in the following way: "A time when it becomes us, and is our wisdom and duty, to keep silence . . . when our speaking would be the casting of pearls before swine . . . but there is also a time to speak for the glory of God and the edification of others . . . and it is a great part of Christian prudence to know when to speak and when to hold our peace."

For the single-parent family there will be times when talking about the divorce experience is unnecessary—even detrimental. There also will be times when their experience, if shared with another hurting family, will speed healing to their hurts.

I have learned this in my own experience. There have been many times I would have loved to speak my mind about my divorce experience, but I knew if I did, nothing positive would result. One instance which stands out in my mind illustrates this.

When I stood before my mother's casket and faced the fifty to sixty members of the church that our family had been asked to leave at the time of my parents' divorce, I wanted to let them know my feelings. I was angry that after twenty-five years of silence while my mother was living, they would appear now to pay honor and respect to my mother's life. I was indignant that those spiritual leaders failed to give me spiritual hope in my hour of need. I wanted to say, "Why are you here? It's too late now." But to do so would have caused more brokenness. In keeping silence I was able to open the door to reconciliation.

However, there are times when I do share what I've experienced. If I failed to speak to churches today about the need to reach out to single-parent families, it would be an even greater failure on my part. My experience tells me these people need the church. If by speaking out I can bring reconciliation, I have spoken for the glory of God and the edification of single-parent families.

When have you recognized the importance of keeping silent? The need to speak out?

A Time to Love

How does the child learn to love God? Isn't it from loving his earthly father?

Parents are the symbol and representative of God's authority to their children. The way parents handle their rulership is the way children will begin to think about God and all other authorities under God. Parents are in a very crucial position in the child's life. Let us look at how a child thinks. If he sees his parents are fair, then he will consider that God must also be fair. If his parents punish for wrong, then God will punish for wrong. If his parents care for him, then God must care for him. If his parents respect and obey God's Word, then he must respect and obey God. If his parents mean what they say, then God must mean what He says.

What about the child who has no father or whose father in no way demonstrates the qualities of our Heavenly Father?

To serve God as he should, that child will need help develop-

171

ing his theology of God. Single-parent mothers can do that by teaching the Word of God and by modeling Christ-like characteristics. Christian male role models can help the single mother also.

This is the way Timothy, a child with apparently no Christian father, developed his knowledge of God (Acts 16:1). Paul the apostle became Timothy's spiritual father and led him into a relationship with God (2 Timothy 1:2).

If you are a single-parent mother, how have you attempted to provide role modeling for your children?

What solid, committed Christian males are available to you to assist in this area with your children?

A Time for Peace

How can the child of divorce make peace with what has happened? How can he grow through divorce, leave the season of divorce behind, and enter the season of recovery? Peace is a possibility for the single-parent family. I want to close this chapter with the following words:

If you follow my decrees and are careful to obey my commands, I will send you rain in its season, and the ground will yield its crops and the trees of the field their fruit. . . . I will grant peace in the land, and you will lie down and no one will make you afraid. I will remove savage beasts from the land, and the sword will not pass through your country. You will pursue your enemies, and they will fall by the sword before you. . . . I will look on you with favor and make you fruitful and increase your numbers, and I will keep my covenant with you. . . . I will put my dwelling place among you, and I will not abhor you. I will walk among you and be your God, and you will be my people. I am the Lord your God, who brought you out of Egypt so that you would no longer be slaves to the Egyptians; I broke the bars of your yoke and enabled you to walk with heads held high (Leviticus 26:3–4,6–7,9,11–13).

12

Building Positive Relationships

Chapter Focus

You can prevent broken relationships. There is such a thing as "Corningware relationships" that will withstand dropping, banging, flare-ups, and freezes.

What God's Word Says

"If . . . there is any encouragement in Christ, if there is any consolation of love, if there is any fellowship of the Spirit, if any affection and compassion, make my joy complete by being of the same mind, maintaining the same love, united in Spirit, intent on one purpose" (Philippians 2:1–2, NASB).

Vignette

The colony of Virginia, begun in 1584, went through many disappointments during its first years. Disasters threatened its existence. Many of its inhabitants perished by famine, sickness, or war with Indians. Some who found life too hard simply deserted the rest. Violent arguments arose among the leaders, threatening anarchy and abandonment. It seemed the colony could not be a homeland for anyone but the natives.

Then Lord Delaware, sent from England to reestablish the colony in 1610, entered the picture. The early account records this paragraph:

A society so feeble and disordered in its frame required a tender and skillful hand to cherish it, and restore its vigour. This it found in Lord Delaware: he searched into the causes of their misfortunes, as far as he could discover them, amidst the violence of their mutual accusations; but instead of exerting his power in punishing crimes that were past, he employed his prudence in healing their dissensions, and in guarding against repetition of the same fatal errors.

People who have experienced broken relationships are like the colony of Virginia. Every new attempt to build something positive is hindered by some previous disaster. But God can do for us what Lord Delaware did for Virginia. He helps us forget the past, heals the roots of bad relationships, and teaches us how to guard against repeating errors in our new relationships. He makes us whole people, capable of whole relationships.

What a gift! If ever we needed help from God, it's in the area of relationship building after relationship breaking.

It has been said: "Of all the gifts He gives us—the most precious, and at times the most perplexing—are the people in our lives."

Let's take a look at the anatomy of a bad relationship.

I am alone. I have been alone for weeks now. It pains me. I hurt so deeply. Each day brings a newer and larger dimension of loneliness. The person who "should" be with me is away, has been for months, even though we live together daily. I have tried and tried to communicate. The line must have shut down completely, for I am not allowed to say my thoughts anymore.

I am alone. My disappointment tonight is real and will loom large in my mind for weeks, I think. No one appreciates me tonight. I felt pretty—almost beautiful—and happy. At this moment I feel only tears and hurt.

I am alone. Nobody must know. I don't think anybody cares. I am fairly sure he won't care to hear me tonight. Our worlds have turned into tight little balls. Neither of us is open with one another anymore. I think I have tried, but time and time again we end up in fights and more fights.

I am alone, O God. I can never be alive and open again with

these lonely thoughts. I am alone night after night. How much longer can I go on being alone?

And now I'll go take off my pretty new dress. After all, Cinderella had to return to the chimney and soot, didn't she? Only she had a happy ending. I think there are no princes around anymore.

–Author Unknown

Have you felt like this unknown author?

What effect does feeling like this have on future relationships?

Broken relationships and the distress that follows cause us to build "ghetto" relationships in our futures.

A definition of *ghetto* is "a well-defined area with borders beyond which its inhabitants seldom if ever move."

For years my husband and I lived in Chicago, a city known for its ethnic ghettos. Little neighborhoods exist all over the city. Chicagoans quickly learn which streets border which ghettos. One side of the street may be the border for one ghetto, and the other side of the street may border another. The people who live in the ghettos not only raise their families there, they also socialize, shop, and work there. Their children marry within the ghetto and begin to raise their families there. Their entire lives are spent isolated in one small area of the huge city of Chicago.

That describes a ghetto relationship also. Because of a person's prior ill-treatment, the walls have gone up and every new relationship is entered into with the intent of maintaining those walls. If the walls are threatened, it is preferable to build them higher—even at the cost of the relationship—rather than tear them down.

Have you built any "ghetto" relationships?

How do you recognize that you have?

What are the walls you have erected?

When continuing a relationship would mean tearing down the walls, what has been your response?

We may not be able to do anything at this point about the relationships which already have been broken, but we can learn to take down our ghetto walls.

Jesus is our role model for relationship building. Before we even begin to talk about building a relationship, He is also our role model for becoming the right person for a relationship. It is much more important to *become* the right person for a relationship than to *find* the right person for a relationship.

In Luke 2:52 we see a picture of Jesus as a whole person, ready for relationship building: "Jesus grew in wisdom, and stature, and in favor with God and men."

Jesus developed five areas of his life to prepare for relationship building. These five areas must be whole in our lives also.

1. "Wisdom"

Jesus was intellectually developed. He had mature thought processes, and a healthy awareness of who He was.

2. "Stature"

He was sound physically. This doesn't mean absence of disease as much as it means absence of negative response to His physical self. He was not a hypochondriac. He knew how to handle physical and emotional stress without it handling him. He took care of himself and was content with His physical being.

3. "In Favor with God"

He was fully-developed spiritually. His relationship with His Father was the reference point for every other relationship He had. He was all God wanted Him to be spiritually.

4. "In Favor with Man"—I

He was mature emotionally. He understood His emotions and knew their positive use in relationship building. He avoided their negative power in causing destructive relationships.

5. "In Favor with Man"—II

He was also socially mature. He knew how to be a true friend and how to socialize in a healthy way. His social mechanisms were finely tuned and carried out through a triangle relationship with self, friend, and God.

If we are rigid and inflexible in any of these areas, we are in a "ghetto" relationship.

How have you matured in these five areas since your broken relationship?

a. Intellectually

b. Physically

c. Spiritually

d. Emotionally

e. Socially

How do you need to mature in these five areas?

a. Intellectually

b. Physically

c. Spiritually

d. Emotionally

e. Socially

Factors That Build Ghetto Walls in Relationships

To be whole in these areas, we need to look at some of the factors which create ghetto relationships. Most of these areas are defenses against being hurt. Most of them will hinder us from developing the kind of relationships Jesus did.

Using the ratio scale after each of the following points, rate your expectations in these areas (1 being "not at all," and 10 being "all the time"):

Fear that the more a person finds out about you, the less they will love you

1—2—3—4—5—6—7—8—9—10

A feeling of worthlessness causes us to build a wall to keep people from really getting to know us. The Bible teaches us to "love your neighbor as yourself." But the by-product of a broken, rejected relationship is often self-hatred. Unless we love ourselves we can never trust another person to really know us. In a

healthy relationship the people who love us really do know us—
and love us anyway.

*Fear that when someone realizes how imperfect you are they will
cease to love you*

1—2—3—4—5—6—7—8—9—10

Because perfection exists only in God, there is no person alive
who can achieve it. But this wall is sometimes so strong that
rather than waiting for someone to discover you are imperfect
you back away from the relationship first.

Desire to find someone who will complete you

1—2—3—4—5—6—7—8—9—10

There are no "missing halves" floating around looking for you.
God didn't create half-people and send them on a major search
to find the other half-person He meant to make you whole. We
must be complete in Christ. If we are not a whole person, we
will not be able to have a whole relationship.

*Desire to have the perfect relationship that will never allow dis-
agreements or criticisms*

1—2—3—4—5—6—7—8—9—10

The perfect relationship doesn't exist. At least it doesn't exist
without its imperfect moments. Anger, criticism, and disagree-
ment are part of every relationship. You will get mad at me and
I will get mad at you. You will disappoint me and I will disappoint you. How we handle our anger and disappointment is the
key to our continuing healthy relationship.

*Belief that the one who is in a close relationship with me will
automatically meet my needs, anticipate my desires, and magi-
cally grant my wishes*

1—2—3—4—5—6—7—8—9—10

No one can do that for you. The greatest need most of us have
is to learn to communicate our needs. Even if we do, no one can
meet all of them. The biblical principle that applies here is looking to God for all our needs, desires, and wishes. He may direct

our loved one to meet the need, but our focus must remain on Him.

Building Positive Relationships

For building positive relationships, we once again turn to Jesus as our role model. His examples of relationship building can be plainly seen in at least four different areas:

1. Jesus had a positive, healthy relationship with His Father. "The Son can do nothing by himself; he can do only what he sees his Father doing, because whatever the Father does the Son also does. For the Father loves the Son and shows him all He does" (John 5:19–20). In the same way, we need to form a close relationship with God.

2. Jesus maintained a positive, healthy disposition toward His earthly family. In becoming a whole, mature adult, Jesus learned how to release himself from his earthly family. He untied the apron strings; He didn't break them. "When Jesus saw his mother there, and the disciple whom he loved standing nearby, he said to his mother, 'Dear woman, here is your son,' and to the disciple, 'Here is your mother.' From that time on, this disciple took her into his home" (John 19:26–27).

3. Jesus had a positive, healthy relationship with His friends. In John 15:15, Jesus tells us, "I have called you friends, for everything that I have learned from my Father I have made known to you."

Jesus had many close friends. He was particularly close to Lazarus, Martha, and Mary. He visited their home regularly, often staying overnight or dropping in for a meal. (We can understand a little better Martha's concern about meal preparation when we realize that when Jesus dropped by, He brought at least twelve people with Him.)

He was also close to John, often called "the beloved disciple." A strong love existed between them that stood the tests of confrontation, disappointment, and misunderstanding.

4. Jesus had a positive, healthy relationship with His acquaintances. The leper who returned to thank Jesus for his healing, the woman at the well of Samaria, the woman taken in adultery (note Luke 8:1–3), and Zacchaeus, the despised tax collector, were each enriched by their acquaintance with Jesus.

Even the brief meeting that the thief on the cross had with Jesus was adequate to transform the final moments of his lawless life into victory.

Write a brief description of your relationship in the four areas mentioned. Where do you need to improve your relationships?

God:

Family:

Friends:

Acquaintances:

Perhaps the door that locks tight our walls of ghetto relationships is the door of qualified love. Unqualified love is not easy for any of us to either give or receive. We often place qualifications on the love we are willing to express:

"If your performance measures up to my expectations, I will be willing to express my love to you as your reward."

"If I don't qualify my love for you, I won't be able to be in control of the relationship."

"If I don't hold back a measure of my expression of love to you, I won't have anything to retaliate with if you disappoint me."

"I'll accept you totally when you meet my expectations of our relationship totally."

Principles of a Good Relationship

We need to learn some principles to aid us in building successful and fulfilling relationships. These principles are listed in Philippians 2:1–2. If we can learn to establish our relationships with these eight principles in mind, our relationships will be great and fulfilling.

Encourage One Another

Encourage means "to inspire with courage." By our conduct, we should inspire each person we have a relationship with to be a better person.

This encouragement has been an important element of the relationship my husband and I have. Because of his past, Jim was not sure for years that he would ever be able to fulfill God's call to enter the pastorate. For those first years I was privileged to be able to inspire him with courage to believe that if God had called him to the ministry, then God knew when and where he should begin.

On the other hand, I timidly stepped into the role of writer when I realized someone had to do what was needed in the area of recovery curricula for children of divorce. Jim inspired me continually, gave me the courage to keep trying, bragged on what I did, and caused me to go forward.

Encouragement inspires the courage to change. Every relationship we enter, if it's going to go anywhere, will likely require change of some kind.

How has someone encouraged you?

Who do you need to encourage?

183

Console One Another

We all have heard there are two things we can count on in life: death and taxes. Unfortunately, there are some other things as well: failure, pain, tragedy, disappointment. When these things occur, we need someone to comfort and console us.

My son entered the sensitive junior high era a few years ago. One day at school a close friend hurt him deeply with a careless remark, pointing out a "defect" which already bothered Jimmy greatly. Jimmy told me about it on the way home from school in the car. He was quite emotional. Upon hearing him, Dinah, our six-year-old, grew unusually quiet. I could see in the rearview mirror that she was sad and troubled. When we arrived home Jimmy walked dejectedly into the house. Dinah caught up to him, threw her arms around him, and, with tears streaming down her little cheeks, said, "Jimmy, I just hate it when someone hurts your feelings." That's "consolation of love." It desires to take the pain away from you. It does whatever it can to build you up. It may not solve the problem, but it definitely tries to help you through the pain.

When have you been consoled in love?

What effect did it have on you?

Fellowship with One Another

The Early Church shared a fellowship of spirit that went far beyond the "let's get together for coffee" kind of socializing we do.

Acts 2:44–47 tells us a little about that fellowship:

All the believers were together and had everything in common. Selling their possessions and goods, they gave to anyone as he had need. Every day they continued to meet together in the temple courts. They broke bread in their homes and ate together with glad and sincere hearts, praising God and enjoying the favor of all the people.

Notice the response of the townspeople around them who were watching this kind of relationship building taking place: 0"The Lord added to their number daily" (Acts 2:47).

Such relationships have been bonded by the Holy Spirit.

It's not easy to tear down the "ghetto walls" to allow this deep fellowshipping to happen. If I want to be one with you in spirit, I must become vulnerable to you, depend upon you, and allow you to know me so well that only by mutual trust could the bond be preserved.

For this reason, it is important to take care in selecting the person you would commune with so deeply. Many Christian singles feel "any old Christian will do!" We are so careful not to be "unequally yoked" with unbelievers, yet we can be just as unequally yoked with a believer. God must begin, establish, and glue these relationships together.

List the names of your friends and acquaintances.

Now circle those with whom you share a true "fellowship of the spirit."

Which of the other people would you like to get to know better? What can you do about it?

Be Affectionate and Compassionate

Affection has nothing to do with romance! It is caring that can exist in any relationship at many different levels. Yet it is something often missing in "ghetto relationships." Compassion sees pain and tries to ease it. Both affection and compassion solve problems in relationships, rather than create problems.

Jesus' ministry on earth was filled with these two qualities. They are especially evident in His dealing with the woman taken in adultery (see John 8). The Pharisees, on the other hand, used people ruthlessly in their attempts to trap Jesus. It was no accident that they had caught the woman "in the act." And though they could have handled the matter privately, they were indifferent to her humiliation and shame. Seeing her plight, Jesus did not back down. With just a few well-chosen words He put her accusers to flight and then released her to her own conscience. When someone cries out for our help, we need to be willing to communicate affection and compassion, not calculate our response.

Describe the last encounter you had where someone touched you with affection and compassion.

Who needs you to touch them right now with affection and compassion?

Be of the Same Mind

This doesn't mean two people share one mind! Neither does it mean two people think the same thoughts all the time.

What this means is that in a good relationship based on these spiritual principles, harmony will exist in the midst of differences.

The more "like-mindedness" in your relationship, the greater its ability to handle differences. At the same time, since growth in a relationship is stimulated by intermingling viewpoints, there is greater growth potential in a relationship that involves the meeting of the minds.

Think of your strongest relationship. Share the ways that "like-mindedness" added vibrancy and growth to that relationship.

Now think about your worst relationship. How did you fail to bring the principle of like-mindedness into that relationship?

Maintain the Same Love

Maintaining love in relationships takes a whole lot of effort.

Soon after moving to Florida, Jim and I discovered we shared an interest in gardening and landscaping. We spent a very enjoyable summer completely redoing the landscape in our yard, both front and back. It was easy to do. It seemed as though every time we passed a nursery we bought a new flower or shrub to add to the landscape.

We still spend time in our garden. If we want to maintain

that beautiful landscape we have to pour hours and hours of work into it: Some weeds in Florida grow through concrete! Insects and disease that threaten the life of flowers and shrubs must be dealt with. And, of course, watering and fertilizing. We even have to tuck our palms under their blankets on a cold night. The list goes on and on.

The Bible gives us a prime example of a relationship which became broken because the two men involved failed to "maintain the same love." It is recorded in Acts, chapter 15.

The apostle Paul and his young friend John Mark entered into a friendship that was close and fulfilling. But during their ministry in Pamphylia, John Mark became sick and suffered from the emotional effects of hardship and persecution.

At this point of the relationship the apostle Paul could not take down the "ghetto walls" of qualified love based on performance. Acts 15:38 reads: "Paul did not think it wise to take him [John Mark], because he had deserted them in Pamphylia and had not continued with them in the work." Paul and John Mark parted company. The relationship broke and remained unreconciled for a period of time. Mark hadn't measured up to Paul's standards, and Paul found that difficult to accept.

Paul did learn to take down those walls of qualified love. The Bible gives the wonderful example of his relationship with Timothy, a young single mother's son. Through that relationship we learn how to "maintain love" in tough times.

What ghetto walls hinder you from remaining in tough relationships?

How far are you willing to let someone go in tearing down those walls?

What can you do to see that they come down?

Be Intent on One Purpose

How can two people from different backgrounds with different strengths and weaknesses, different life-experiences, and different personalities meet and learn to care deeply about one another without losing their own uniqueness?

How can they be intent on expressing and caring for that other person and still grow and develop individually?

They do it by becoming intent on the one purpose God wants them to accomplish: to make their relationship a conduit through which His love flows into them and out of them to those around them.

God has a special reason for birthing every "Philippians 2" relationship we find. We must bond with that other person in such a way that we allow God to develop the relationship according to His purposes.

Paul and Barnabas had a "Philippians 2" relationship. Their common goal and design was to reach the world for God.

But the rift between John Mark and Paul also damaged the relationship between Paul and Barnabas. They took their eyes off their goals and put them on their differences.

Note: It is only as we look ahead to the design God has for our relationships that we can maintain them.

Relationship building—tearing down ghetto walls—depends on these eight principles.

Holding onto another person in a relationship depends on letting go of his (or her) hand to take the hand of Christ, and allowing Him to take his (or her) hand.

Such a relationship triangle allows God's Spirit to flow freely through my open spirit to you. It allows me to love you as myself.

List ways you see to develop a closer union with your friends according to the eight biblical principles we have studied in this chapter.

13

Discovering Your Design

Chapter Focus

God has a design for your life. Not only can you discover what His design for you is, you can take steps that will allow that design to be worked out in your life.

What God's Word Says

"All the days ordained for me were written in your book before one of them came to be" (Psalm 139:16).

"He has made everything beautiful in its time. He has also set eternity in the hearts of men; yet they cannot fathom what God has done from beginning to end" (Ecclesiastes 3:11).

Vignette

> Humpty Dumpty sat on a wall.
> Humpty Dumpty had a great fall.
> All the king's horses, and all the king's men
> Couldn't put Humpty Dumpty together again!

Many people who go through the crisis of loss by divorce develop "Humpty Dumpty" complexes. Like Humpty Dumpty, they desperately want to be "put back together again." But sadly, like that nursery rhyme character, real people are not looking in the right places for repair. The "king's men" of our world—psychology, medicines, secular therapies, and other such remedies—do not contain the "glue" to do the job any more than did the king's men of the nursery rhyme. But God does.

Psalm 139:16 tells us that all our days are ordained before we are even born. And with all of their delight—and distress— they are beautiful (Ecclesiastes 3:11). In fact, all things that happen to us, good, bad, or indifferent, are the very events God ordained as necessary and profitable to make us into the person He intended.

Yet from our finite position in the mid-stream of life, it seems that we are broken apart by the onrush of events. It is especially at those times that we must remember who the Master Architect is! Just because we can't make sense of the broken pieces of our lives doesn't mean He can't. It just means that we are going to have to trust God to show us the beauty of this time and to remind us of His ordination of our days.

Then we have to trust Him enough to let Him apply the "glue" that puts us together in the ways, and at the times, that He determines are best.

Keeping this poem in mind will help:

As children bring their broken toys with tears for us to mend,
I brought my broken dreams to God because He was my friend.
But then, instead of leaving Him in peace to work alone,
I hung around and tried to help in ways that were my own.
At last I snatched them back and cried, "How can you be so slow?"
"My child," He said, "What could I do? You never did let go!"
—Author Unknown

Nothing can alter God's original design for your life. We get the idea sometimes that it is changed by adverse circumstances. That isn't so. Sometimes we move out of the plan God has for our lives, but at any moment He can bring us right back into His original design for our lives if we will let Him do it.

Using the chart on the next page list both the positive and negative factors you feel have made you who you are today.

Positive Factors	Negative Factors

Answer these questions:

How can I know the plan of my life?

How much of it has been determined?

How much of it has been changed by negative experiences in my life?

.

An interesting truth of Ecclesiastes 3:11 is this: Even though we may feel like our lives have been broken into a million pieces and our dreams have been shattered, we can't see as God sees. We "cannot fathom what God has done from beginning to end."

Job went through enough to qualify him to speak to us, and this is what he concluded: "I know that you can do all things; no plan of yours can be thwarted" (Job 42:2).

Let's develop a concept that will help us overcome our Humpty Dumpty viewpoints.

There are three important things to remember about God's plan for your life.

1. It is *His* plan. And you are to work with God to discover and own that plan for yourself.

2. His plan for you is unique, tailored to you. Though others may have faced circumstances similar, perhaps (as far as you can see) identical to yours, no one else has ever had an identical plan.

3. You must discover His plan, and develop it in your life.

Think about the dead ends you have hit in your personal life. Make a list of what you already know is not God's plan for your life.

In thinking about your life, make a list of the times and ways you think you may have moved out of God's plan for your life.

It isn't always easy to think about life's difficulties, is it? But to begin a positive search for God's plan for your life you have to learn first to face the setbacks, the reverses. I learned that with the birth of our third child, Dinah. Before Dinah was born, my husband, Jim, and I thought we were finished with our family. We had one boy and one girl, a perfect arrangement given our busy life-style in the ministry.

All at once we realized that even though we may have finished—apparently God wasn't. A third child was on the way. I wondered how I could ever handle another baby. I figured the forty thousand diapers or so I had already used with the first two were more than enough for me to change. I was afraid a new baby would disrupt my busy life. I was busy with our church ministry to single adults. In addition to that I was traveling to conduct single-parent family seminars and using whatever spare time I could find to write.

Being aware of the power of prayer, I prayed: "God, since a new baby is definitely on the way, please make it perfect." Then, caught up in the inspiration of the moment, I continued, "And even let this baby come potty trained."

The day in March came when Dinah was born. Shortly after the doctor laid her in my arms, I was faced with the fact that God had not answered all my prayers. Dinah let me know she was not potty trained.

I could have responded in one of two ways: I could have resented the reality of the situation. Or I could become grateful that there was such a thing as disposable diapers. I chose the latter.

That opportunity is presented to us every time we recognize a negative circumstance in our lives. We can choose to walk on one of two paths: the path God planned for us to follow or our own path into negativism.

Let's begin following the path to God's design for you and me. Consider the following Scripture portion:

> We know that in all things God works for the good of those who love him, who have been called according to his purpose. For those God foreknew he also predestined to be conformed to the likeness of his Son, that he might be the firstborn among many brothers. And those he predestined, he also called; those he called, he also justified; those he justified, he also glorified (Romans 8:28–30).

Within all that theological terminology we can discover the path to God's design for our lives. The key words from this Scripture passage that we need to look at more closely are these: "good," "foreknew," "predestined," "called," "justified," and "glorified."

Look at the verses of Scripture again. Do these words have any relevance for your life? If so, in what ways?

Good:

195

Foreknew:

Predestined:

Called:

Justified:

Glorified:

If all things "work together for the good" in us, then what is "the good"?

Finding God's Design

The phrase "all things work together for good" has been quoted over and over again. It becomes the all-purpose promise, the knot in the end of the rope we're supposed to hang onto, the "justification" for anyone's reaction to our circumstances.

The key to understanding this verse is realizing that while we are the ones for whom this verse was written, God is the one who determines what the good is. The next verse tells us what the good is: "to be conformed to the likeness of his Son." This is our ultimate design. When we recognize the way to it, it will make us more like Jesus Christ.

When we feel broken and defeated by life, all we have to do is trust the Lord to get us back to the fork in the road where we began to walk a path of our own design. When we get back on His path for our lives, we will discover that He will once again conform us to His image.

The first step is to be sure we are on the right path, where God can conform us to the image of His Son. That's real "designer living."

The second step is realizing God has "set eternity in [our] hearts," as the writer of Ecclesiastes (3:11) tells us. *The Living Bible* paraphrases Psalm 139:16 this way, "You saw me before I was born and scheduled each day of my life before I began to breathe."

We struggle with the meaning of the word "foreknew." All it means is that God knew me before. Before what? Before my plans for my life, before broken dreams, before hurtful events, before broken relationships, before childhood disappointments, before birth.

Unfortunately, the brokenness we experience can make us feel separated from God. So how do we get back to God? How do we get back on the right path? How do we begin to be conformed to the image of Christ? It's no big secret. It is God's plan that everybody would know the answer to those important questions.

"For those he did foreknow he also did predestine . . . and those he did predestine, he also called." The two words to consider are "predestined" and "called." Let's consider the meaning of these two words according to one dictionary.

Predestine, predestinate—"To predetermine or foreordain; to appoint or ordain beforehand by an unchangeable purpose."

Called—"Invited; summoned; addressed; named; appointed; invoked; assembled by order."

We begin to be shaped into the image of Christ, the design we were appointed to by God before we ever came to be. And God's design is an unchangeable design to which we have all been appointed to. This appointed purpose is for every person who has ever lived. Romans 3 tells us about it: "All have turned away, they have together become worthless; there is no one who does good, not even one . . . all have sinned and fall short of the glory of God, and are justified freely by his grace through the redemption that came by Christ Jesus" (vv. 12,23–24).

197

God has an unchangeable purpose for us that began before our birth. He has invited us to receive His gift of salvation through Jesus Christ His Son. God's design is for our good, and God foreknew and predestined us to it.

When did you realize you had been invited to receive this gift of salvation?

Describe how it affected you.

"Those he called he also justified. . . ."

With justification God declares us not guilty. Through His Son's own righteousness He gives us the right to stand before Him sinless and forgiven.

In another chapter we talked about the wonderful therapy of God's forgiveness. When we find ourselves back on God's path and accept His forgiveness, by His reckoning we never left His road. We don't have a right to feel guilty after God has forgiven us. But many times we do.

All that God knows about your sins and failures has been recorded in the space below.

Don't you dare look at that empty space and picture what you think should be listed there. God has no memory of your sin. He has taken your past away. You don't have a right to it!

"Those he justified he also glorified." That thought ought to permeate our thinking, dispelling our feelings of worthlessness. God has filled us with Christ's goodness. We have become a mirror-image of Him. He put us back on the path to our ultimate design. He promises to have the greatest surprise of all waiting for us when we reach His glory.

The most important thought is this: We have to see ourselves as that "mirror image" to discover His design!

God's original design for your life has not been altered in any way by the circumstances of your life. You must believe that to see it.

Producing Fruit of the Spirit

God plants the seed, but we produce the fruit. Since our unique design was established before we were born, many of our unique characteristics are going to be used to shape our lives. We have to find out how to use the positive characteristics and discard the negative ones.

The New Testament teaches us about positive and negative characteristics.

When you follow your own wrong inclinations your lives will produce these evil results: impure thoughts, eagerness for lustful pleasure, idolatry, spiritism (that is, encouraging the activity of demons), hatred and fighting, jealousy and anger, constant effort to get the best for yourself, complaints and criticisms, the feeling that everyone else is wrong except those in your little group—and there will be wrong doctrine, envy, murder, drunkenness, wild parties, and all that sort of thing. Let me tell you again as I have before, that anyone living that sort of life will not inherit the kingdom of God.

But when the Holy Spirit controls our lives, he will produce this kind of fruit in us: love, joy, peace, patience, kindness, goodness, faithfulness, gentleness and self-control; and here there is no conflict with Jewish laws (Galatians 5:19–23, *Living Bible*).

The Bible teaches us that our negative characteristics are evidence that we have not allowed God to control that area of our lives.

Galatians 5 is a key portion of God's Word. It reveals a major

199

feature of God's design for us: It reveals the fruit His design produces in us!

What bad fruit is evidenced in your life?

Jeremiah 10:23–24 says, "O Lord, I know it is not within the power of man to map his life and plan his course—so you correct me, Lord" (*Living Bible*).

Have you asked God to correct your course?

Design a plan for developing each of the following fruits of the Spirit in your own life. Use the Bible references given for each fruit. You probably will want to list the negative characteristics you possess that can be supplanted by these fruit. Set goals for ways to nourish the Spirit's fruit in your life.

Love

"Dear friends, let us love one another, for love comes from God. Everyone who loves has been born of God and knows God" (1 John 4:7).
"Love the Lord your God with all your heart and with all your soul and with all your mind and with all your strength" (Mark 12:30).

Joy

"The ransomed of the Lord will return. They will enter Zion with singing; everlasting joy will crown their heads" (Isaiah 35:10).

"You have filled my heart with greater joy than when their grain and new wine abound" (Psalm 4:7).

Peace

"Peacemakers who sow in peace raise a harvest of righteousness" (James 3:18).

"Peace I leave with you; my peace I give you. I do not give to you as the world gives. Do not let your hearts be troubled and do not be afraid" (John 14:27).

"Therefore, since we have been justified through faith, we have peace with God through our Lord Jesus Christ" (Romans 5:1).

Patience

"Be completely humble and gentle; be patient, bearing with one another in love" (Ephesians 4:2).

Kindness

"The Lord's servant must not quarrel; instead, he must be kind to everyone, able to teach, not resentful" (2 Timothy 2:24).

Goodness

"The good man brings good things out of the good stored up in him" (Matthew 12:35).

Faithfulness

"Love the Lord, all his saints! The Lord preserves the faithful, but the proud he pays back in full" (Psalm 31:23).

"Be faithful, even to the point of death, and I will give you the crown of life" (Revelation 2:10).

" 'Well done, my good servant!' his master replied. 'Because you have been trustworthy in a very small matter, take charge of ten cities' " (Luke 19:17).

Gentleness

"Be completely humble and gentle; be patient, bearing with one another in love" (Ephesians 4:2).

Self-Control

"Make every effort to add to your faith goodness; and to goodness, knowledge; and to knowledge, self-control; and to self-control, perseverance; and to perseverance, godliness; and to godliness, brotherly kindness; and to brotherly kindness, love" (2 Peter 1:5–7).

Now develop a chart. Under the column headed "Negative," list the negative characteristics you are still overcoming. Under the column headed, "Positive," write which fruit of the Spirit will help you overcome the negative one. Tell how the process can be completed.

Negative   Positive

It will take consistent work to develop the fruit of the Spirit. Work on it every day. Keep a journal showing your progress. This internal fruit production is crucial to enable us to make the right choices to walk where He leads. The fruit is the description of our internal design. It is the glue that rids us of our Humpty Dumpty complexes. It is the Master Architect's plan to bring us into designer living.

Epilogue

Well, my friend, this book has been successful if it has pointed you to the Christ of your circumstances. If, throughout the pages of this book, you have learned to take your focus off your circumstances and put it on Christ, then my goal has been accomplished.

Even if those negative circumstances never change, Christ is capable of keeping you joyously victorious in the midst of them. His love will gently, graciously guide you into the future He has designed for you.

"The people who survive the sword will find favor in the desert; I will come to give rest to Israel. . . . I have loved you with an everlasting love; I have drawn you with loving-kindness. I will build you up again and you will be rebuilt, O Virgin Israel. Again you will take up your tambourines and go out to dance with the joyful" (Jeremiah 31:2–4).

I recall an interview of Joni Eareckson Tada, a beautiful Christian woman who has spent more than twenty-five years in a wheelchair. She was asked if she didn't have some days when she rebelled against her limitations.

Joni told the interviewer that she kept her perspective on her circumstances by continually saying yes to Jesus. By way of illustration, she spoke of her father's death, which had only recently occurred. Shortly after learning that he had passed away, she was in a shopping mall. Her father's death had not yet hit her emotionally; she had not cried. Then she heard a song being played over the public address system that unleashed those emotions.

"I just started sobbing. I couldn't hide my face in a tissue. I couldn't run to a bathroom. I couldn't bury myself in a clothes rack and get lost and just be private and cry for a moment. There I was, just staring at a mannequin, crying. I said out loud, 'Lord, Jesus, I choose you. I don't choose depression; I don't choose hurt and pain—I choose you.'"

That is what it means to handle daily living: the constant, deliberate choice of saying yes to Jesus—no matter the circumstances.

Endnotes

PAGE

12   "There is nothing . . ." Alan Redpath, *Victorious Christian Living* (Westwood, N.J.: Fleming H. Revell Co., 1955), 166.

13   "In marriage one expects . . ." Joy K. Rice and David G. Rice, *Living Through Divorce: A Developmental Approach to Divorce* (New York: The Guildford Press, 1986), 70.

14   A man experiencing the grief . . . Robert S. Weiss, *Marital Separation* (New York: Basic Books, Inc., 1975), 48.

22   Dr. Elisabeth Kübler-Ross wrote . . . Elisabeth Kübler-Ross, *On Death and Dying* (MacMillan Publishing Co.: New York, 1969), 114.

24   "Something beautiful something good . . ." "Something Beautiful," words by Gloria Gaither; music by William J. Gaither. Copyright 1971 by William J. Gaither. All rights reserved. Used by permission.

25   "The Lord is never nearer . . ." Lloyd John Ogilvie, *Drumbeat of Love* (Waco, Tex.: Word Books, 1976), 23.

28   "I am convinced that depression . . ." Ibid., 24.

41   "A little lady named Irene . . ." Jim Dycus and Barbara Dycus, *Not Guilty! From Convict to Christian: The Jim Dycus Story* (San Francisco, Calif.: Harper and Row, 1988), 97–98.

49   "Rejection hurts, a lot . . ." Bobbie Reed, *Learn to Risk: Finding Joy as a Single Adult* (Grand Rapids, Mich.: Zondervan Publishing House, 1990), 33.

51   "Rag Doll" by Robin Williams. Used by permission.

61   "The pervasiveness of . . ." Judith S. Wallerstein and Joan Berlin Kelly, *Surviving the Breakup: How Children and Parents Cope with Divorce* (New York: Basic Books, 1982), 156.

67   "I hadn't been in the ministry long . . ." Dycus, *Not Guilty,* 139.

67   "Suddenly the issue was no longer important . . ." Ibid., 140.

73   In his book . . . Weiss, *Marital Separation*, 42.

79   "Whatever the mind can conceive . . ." Dale E. Galloway, *Dream a New Dream: How to Rebuild a Broken Life* (Wheaton, Ill.: Tyndale House, 1975), 57.

83   Morton Hunt, Christian psychologist . . . Morton Hunt and Bernice Hunt. *The Divorce Experience* (New York: McGraw-Hill, 1977), 140.

87   "What did I know about dating . . ." Dycus, *Not Guilty,* 117.

94   "I've been bound . . ." Dycus, *Not Guilty,* 2–3.

98   Dwight H. Small says . . . Dwight Hervey Small, *The Right to Remarry* (Old Tappan, N.J.: Fleming H. Revell Company, 1977), 173.

102   "I stayed there . . ." Dycus, *Not Guilty,* 100.

104   "And because she did . . ." Dycus, *Not Guilty,* 116.

107   Dr. Harold Ivan Smith . . . Jason Towner, *Forgiving Is For Giving* (Grand Rapids: Zondervan, 1982), 79.

114   "He Giveth More Grace" by Hubert C. Mitchell, Annie Johnson Flint. Copyright 1941. Renewed 1969, Lillenas Publishing Company/SESAC. All rights reserved. Used by permission of Integrated Copyright Group, Inc.

124   One commentary renders . . . Matthew Henry, *Matthew Henry's Commentary on the Whole Bible* (New York: Fleming H. Revell, Co., n.d.), 996.

125   "Healing for all your hurts . . ." Galloway, *Dream,* 128.

135   Over one million . . . "Kids and Divorce," *Orlando Sentinel*, June 16, 1993.

135   Most of these reactions . . . Neal C. Buchanan and Eugene Chamberlain, *Helping Children of Divorce* (Nashville, Tenn.: Broadman Press, 1981), 20–25. The material on the reactions children experience when faced with parents who are divorced were mentioned in this book. The expansion and explanations for these principles are from the author's own experiences.

146   "For children and adolescents . . ." Wallerstein, *Surviving,* 35–36.

155   "It is not divorce, but the emotional . . ." J. Louise Despert, *Children of Divorce* (New York: Doubleday & Co., 1953), vii.

156   "An authority figure . . ." *What the Bible Says About Child Training* (Tempe, Ariz.: Aletheia Publications, 1980), 39–40.

160   Velma Carter and Lynn Leavenworth, in counseling . . . Velma Thorne Carter and J. Lynn Leavenworth, *Caught in the Middle: Children of Divorce* (Valley Forge, Pa.: Judson Press, 1985), 120–121.

163   "God has established the institution . . ." Fugate, *What the Bible says About Child Training,* 29.

167   "Little children, rejoice . . ." Words by William J. and Gloria Gaither. Music by William J. Gaither. © Copyright 1973 by William J. Gaither. All rights reserved. Used by permission.

168   As Bruce Fisher says . . . Bruce Fisher, *Rebuilding: When Your Relationship Ends* (San Luis Obispo, Calif.: Impact Publishers, 1985), 112.

171   Matthew Henry comments . . . Henry, *Commentary,* 996.

172   "Parents are the symbol . . ." Fugate, *What the Bible Says About Child Training,* 41.

176   "A society so feeble . . ." William Roberson, *History of the Discovery and Settlement of America* (1835), quoted in *Christian History of the Consititution of the United States of America*, ed. Joseph Allan Montgomery, comp. Verna M. Hall (San Francisco, Calif.: The American Christian Constitution Press, 1960), 161.

204   I recall an interview . . . This paraphrase came from an interview with Joni Eareckson Tada, which appeared in the *Orlando Sentinal.*